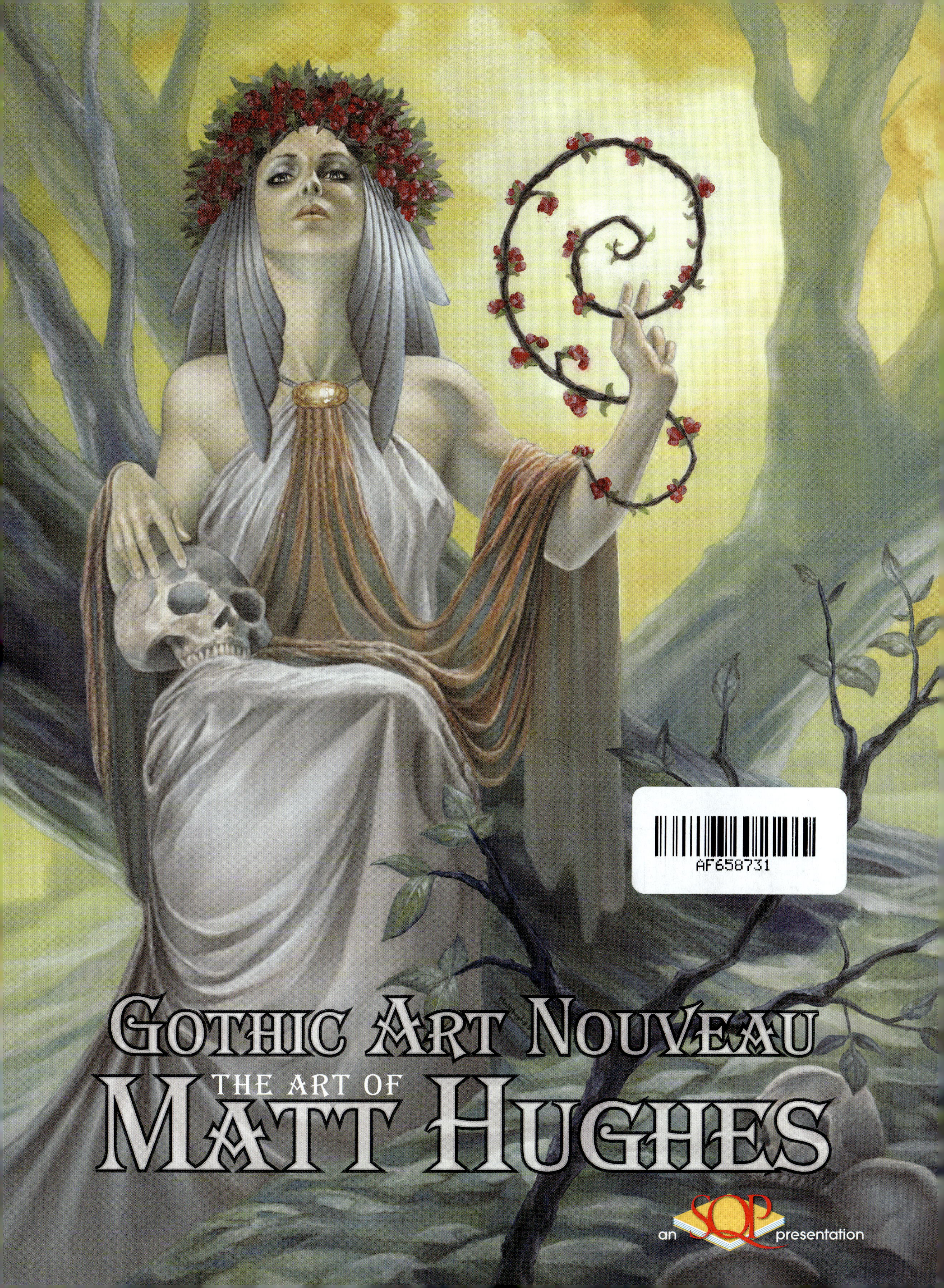

Gothic Art Nouveau

The Art of Matt Hughes

an SQP presentation

Glorious Resplendence

The art of Matt Hughes harkens to a more enchanting age...

An accomplished writer, artist and designer, Matt's work has been shown in galleries throughout the world, and featured in numerous publications such as: *Art Scene International*, *Dark Realms Magazine*, *Realms of Fantasy Magazine*, *Magical Blend Magazine*, *White Wolf Publishing*, *Heavy Metal Magazine*, *Mystique Magazine*, the *Oracle* and *Wizard Magazine*. In addition, several collaborative publications have showcased his work, including *Spectrum*, *Masters of Fantasy*, *How to Draw and Paint Fairies*, *Anatomy for Fantasy Artists* and *Creative Minds*. In 2004, Matt's illustration, *"Boudicca"*, appeared on the cover of a greeting card set given to the *Lord of the Rings* cast and crew at an After Oscar Party, and in that same year, he was honored as a Gallery Winner in the *Society of Illustrators*, LA art competition. In 2007 Matt was honored with Best in Show Award at *DragonCon* and took the role of Art Show Judge the following year. In 2013 Matt was honored with the opportunity to produce three opera posters for the *Atlanta Opera* Season.

Ingeniously blending the romantic aesthetic beauty of Art Nouveau with the dark concepts of Gothic art, painter Matt Hughes is best known for giving rise to Gothic Art Nouveau, a new art movement that's redefining the relationship between viewer and subject, entwining both into an intimate rendezvous, sharing dark and ethereal realms immersed in religion and mythology, death and spirituality, human nature and inherent evil, ultimately leaving the viewer with a profundity of self-reflection and introspection.

Matt's first book, *"Metamorphosis – The Art of Matt Hughes"*, published in 2005 by MG Publishing/SQP, sold over 23,000 copies internationally. He soon followed in 2008 by publishing his second collective works, *"Ethereal Visions – The Art of Matt Hughes"*. Here now is the third collection of his work.

Matt currently resides in Atlanta, GA with his wife and muse, Hope.

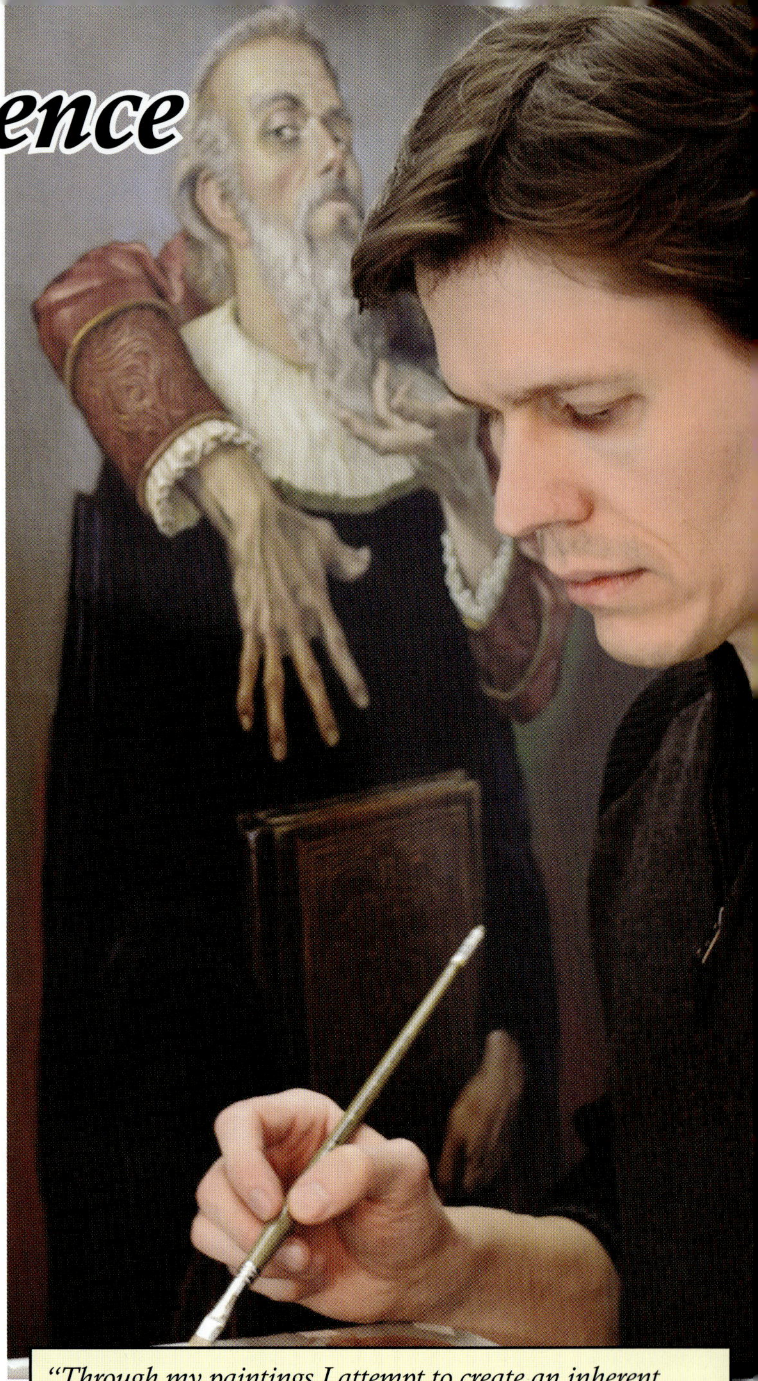

"Through my paintings I attempt to create an inherent language of emotion, truth, lies, and common experiences that will inevitably lead the viewer to personal reflection and a better understanding of self. I utilize this language as a means to elucidate my demons forcing me to come face to face with my own folly of self. The symbolic nature of the elements helps to weave a deeper understanding of cultural influences that are not only self-relevant but also viewer-relevant." – Matt Hughes

I would like to dedicate this book as well as the body of work it represents to my loving and support wife, Hope. Thank you for understanding the insanity that is socks.
– Matt Hughes

To learn more about Matt and his work please visit his website at **www.matthughesart.com**

Gothic Art Nouveau - The Art of Matt Hughes

Book design by Grassy Knoll Studios.

Published by SQP Inc.
PO Box 248 - Columbus NJ 08022

Sal Quartuccio & Bob Keenan - Publishers

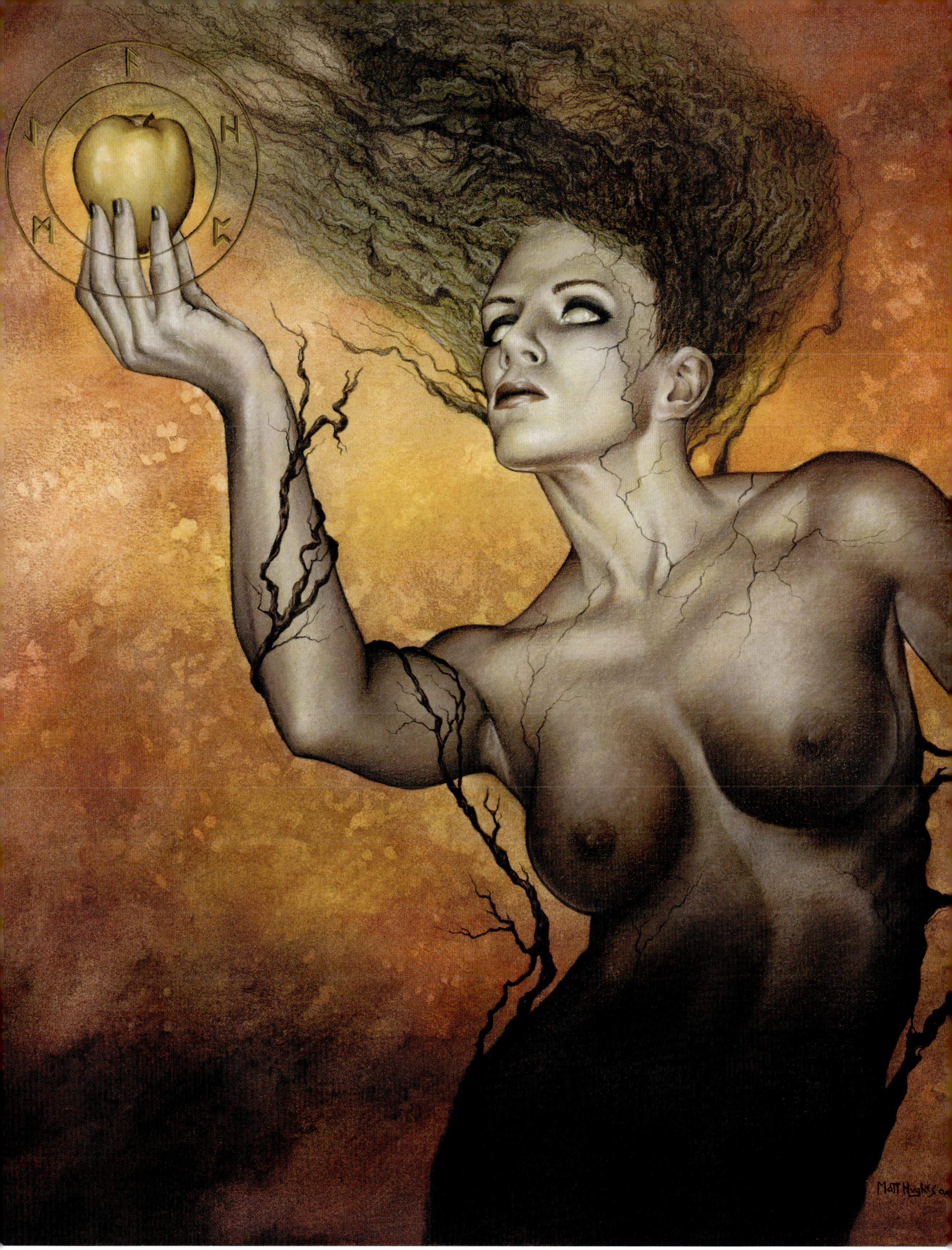

Becoming

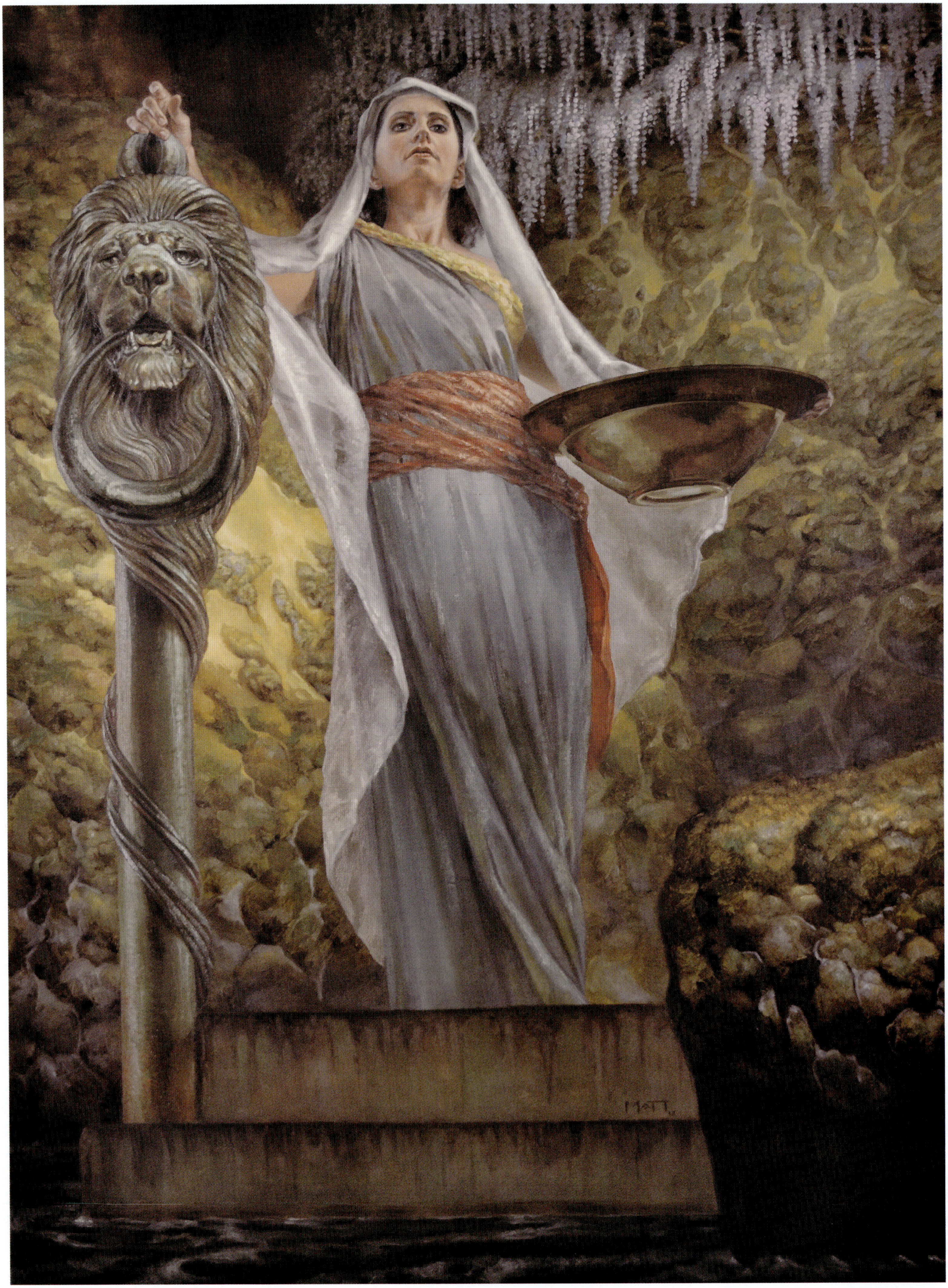

The Edge of Lethe

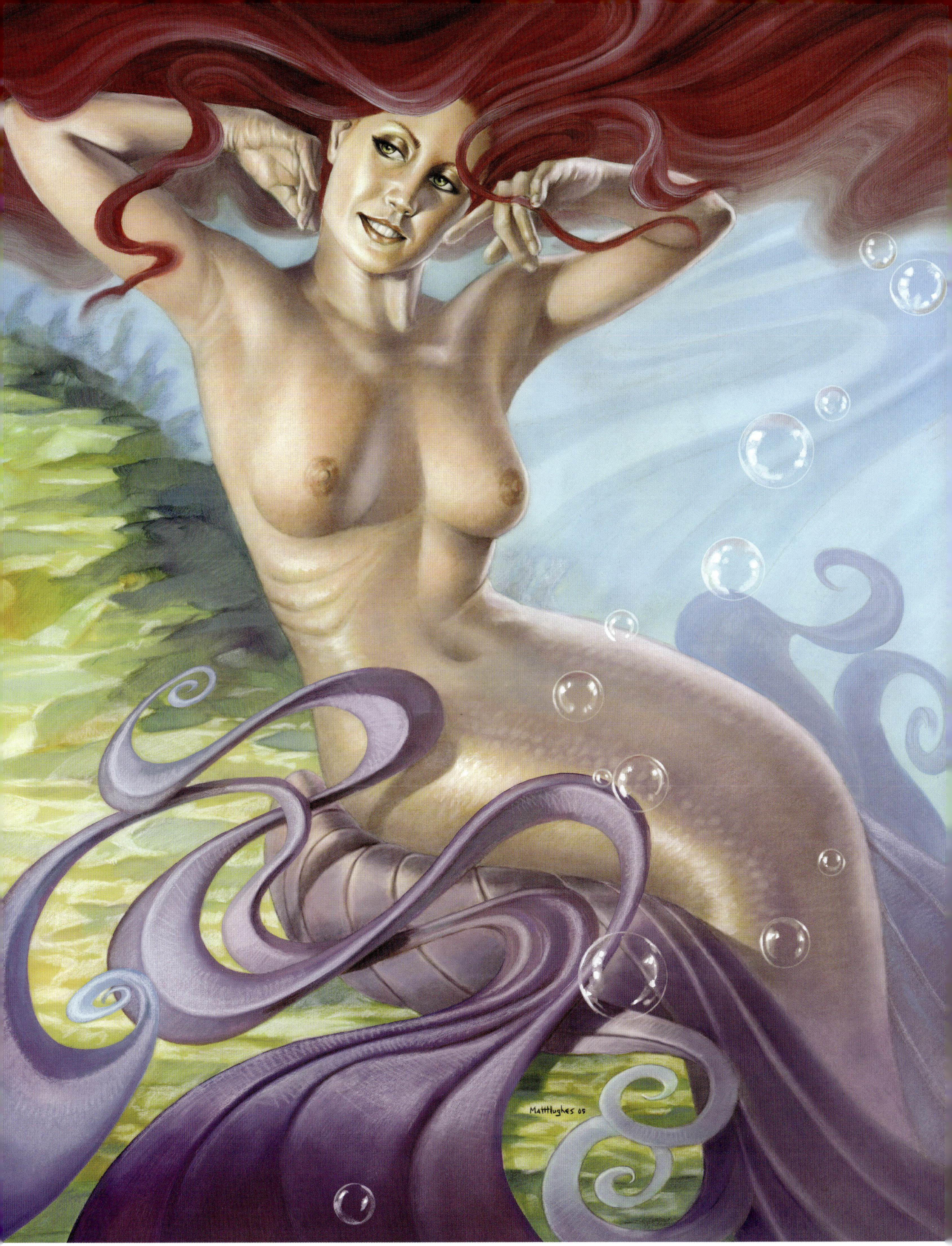

Mermaid

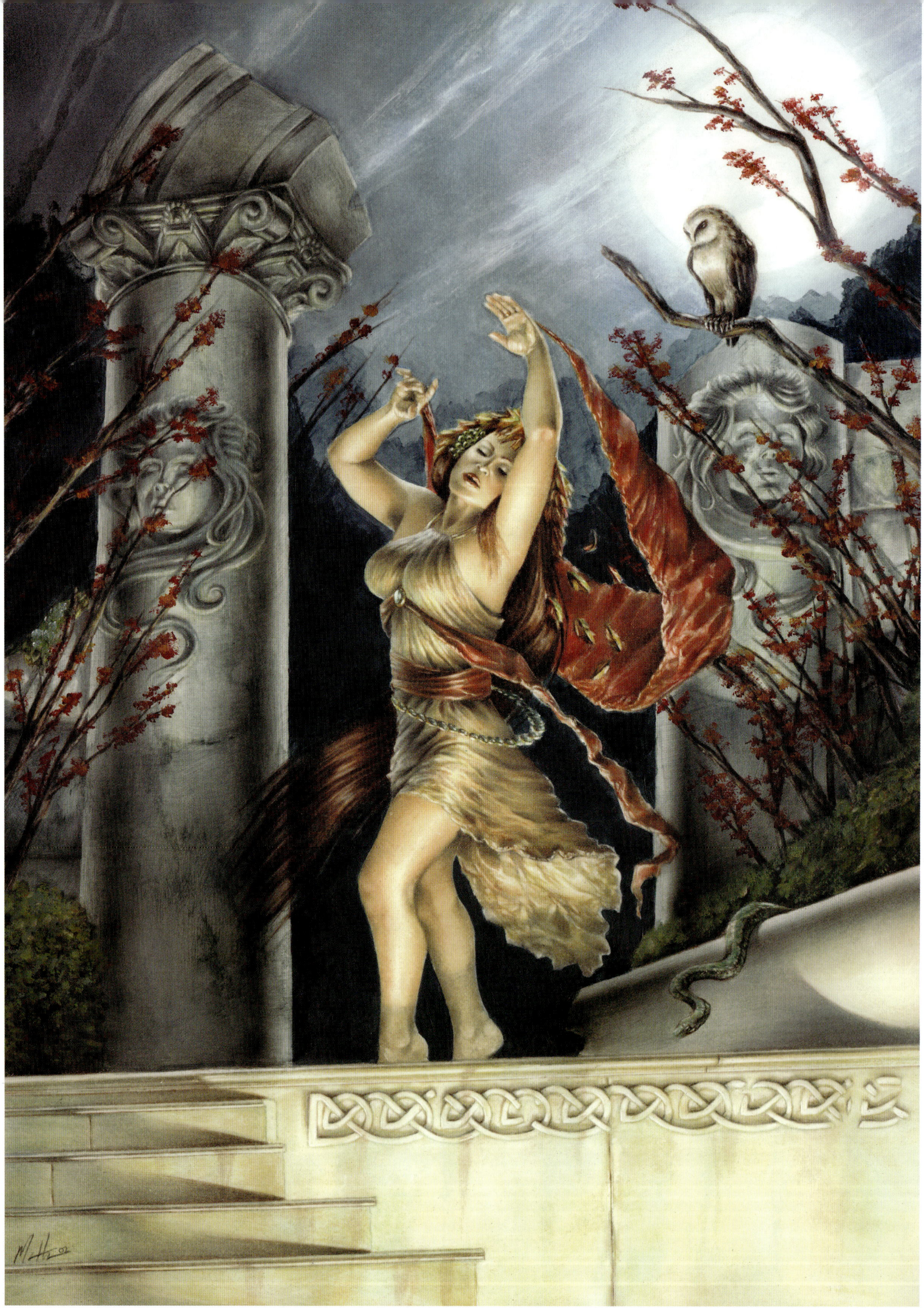

Hecate

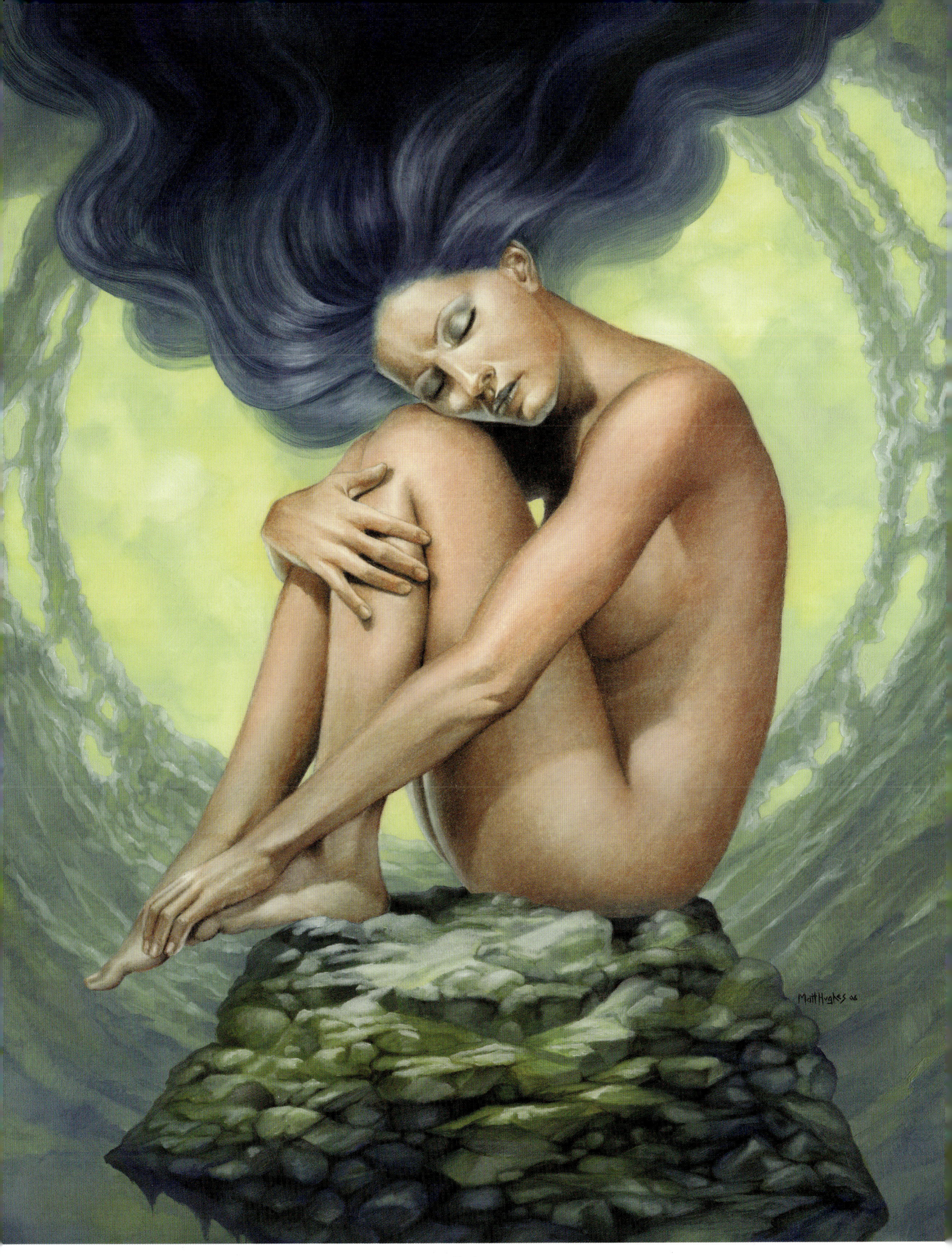

Jade

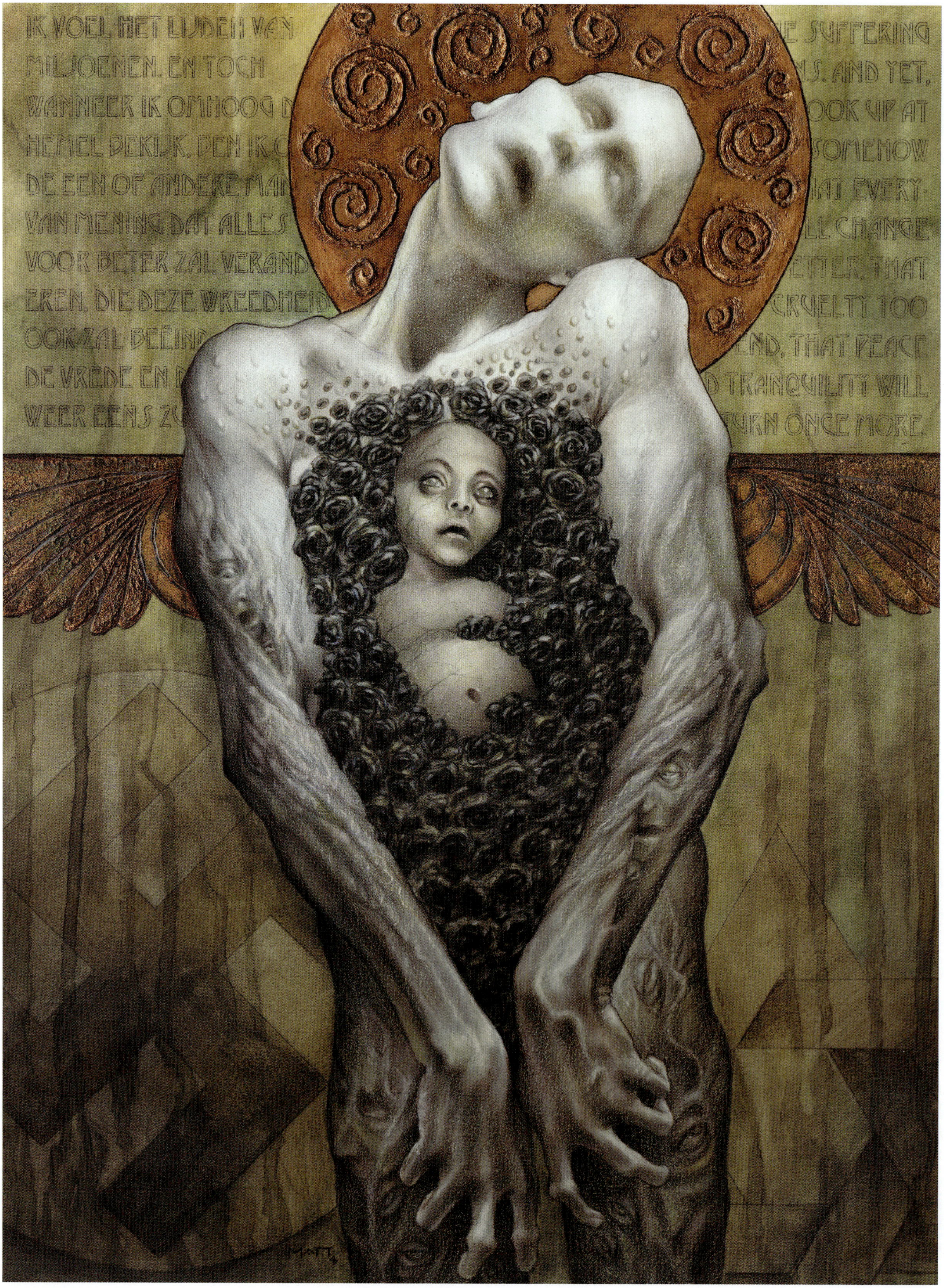
IK VOEL HET LIJDEN VAN
MILJOENEN. EN TOCH
WANNEER IK OMHOOG D
HEMEL BEKIJK, BEN IK O
DE EEN OF ANDERE MAN
VAN MENING DAT ALLES
VOOR BETER ZAL VERAND
EREN, DIE DEZE WREEDHEID
OOK ZAL BEËIND
DE VREDE EN D
WEER EENS ZU
E SUFFERING
NS. AND YET,
OOK UP AT
SOMEHOW
HAT EVERY-
LL CHANGE
ETTER, THAT
CRUELTY TOO
END, THAT PEACE
D TRANQUILITY WILL
TURN ONCE MORE
MATT

Remember

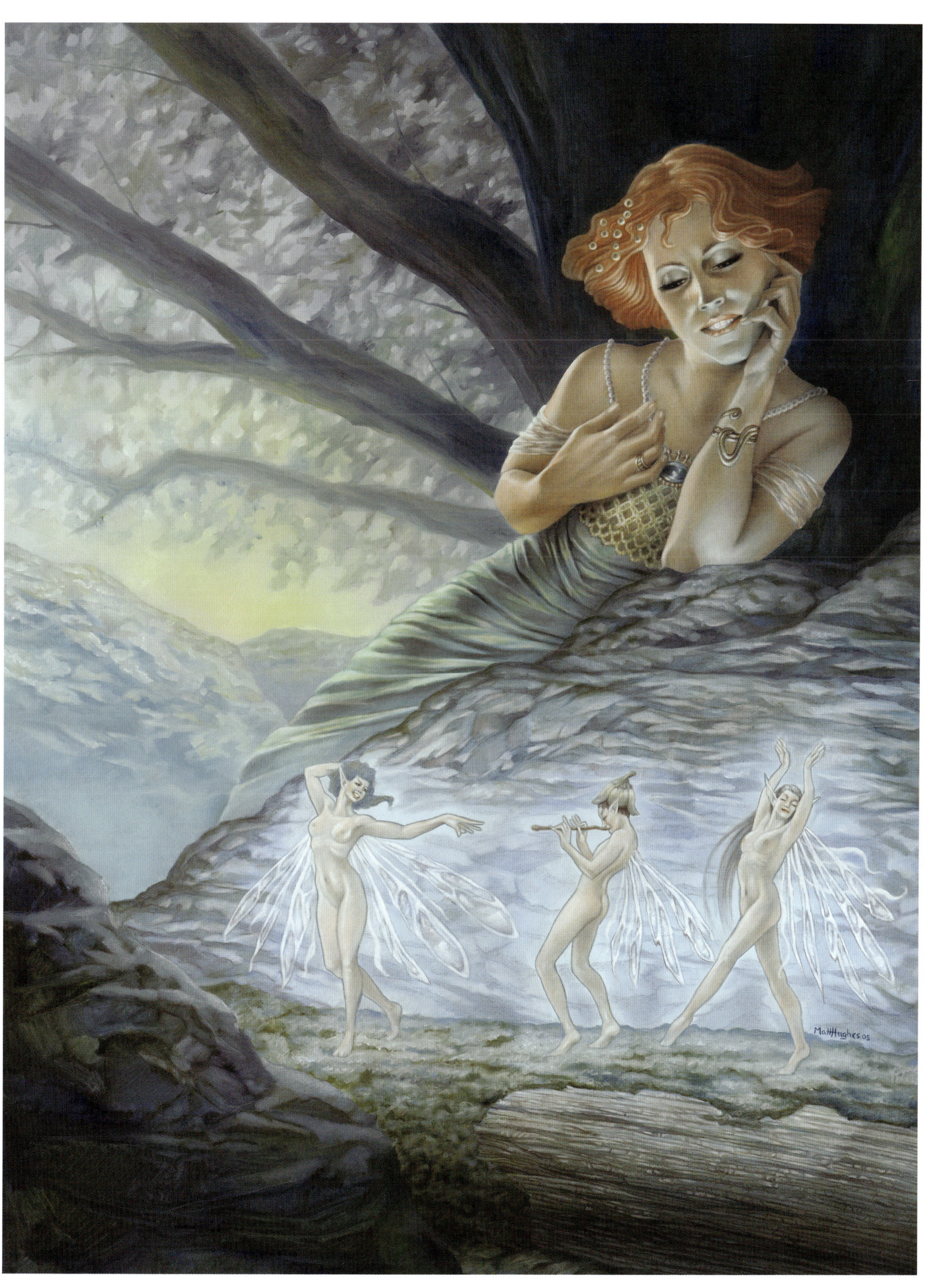

Twilight Waltz

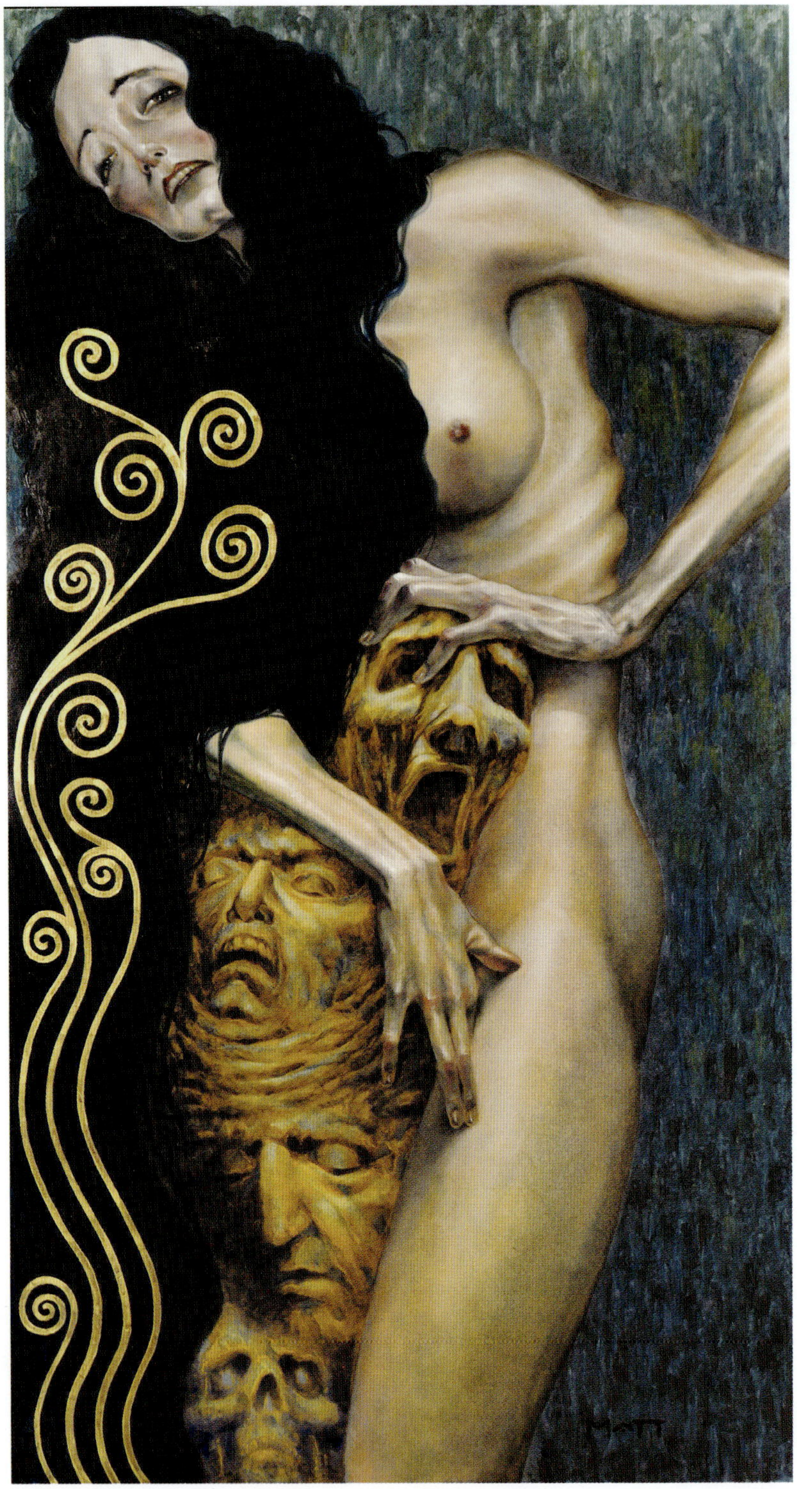

Pandora

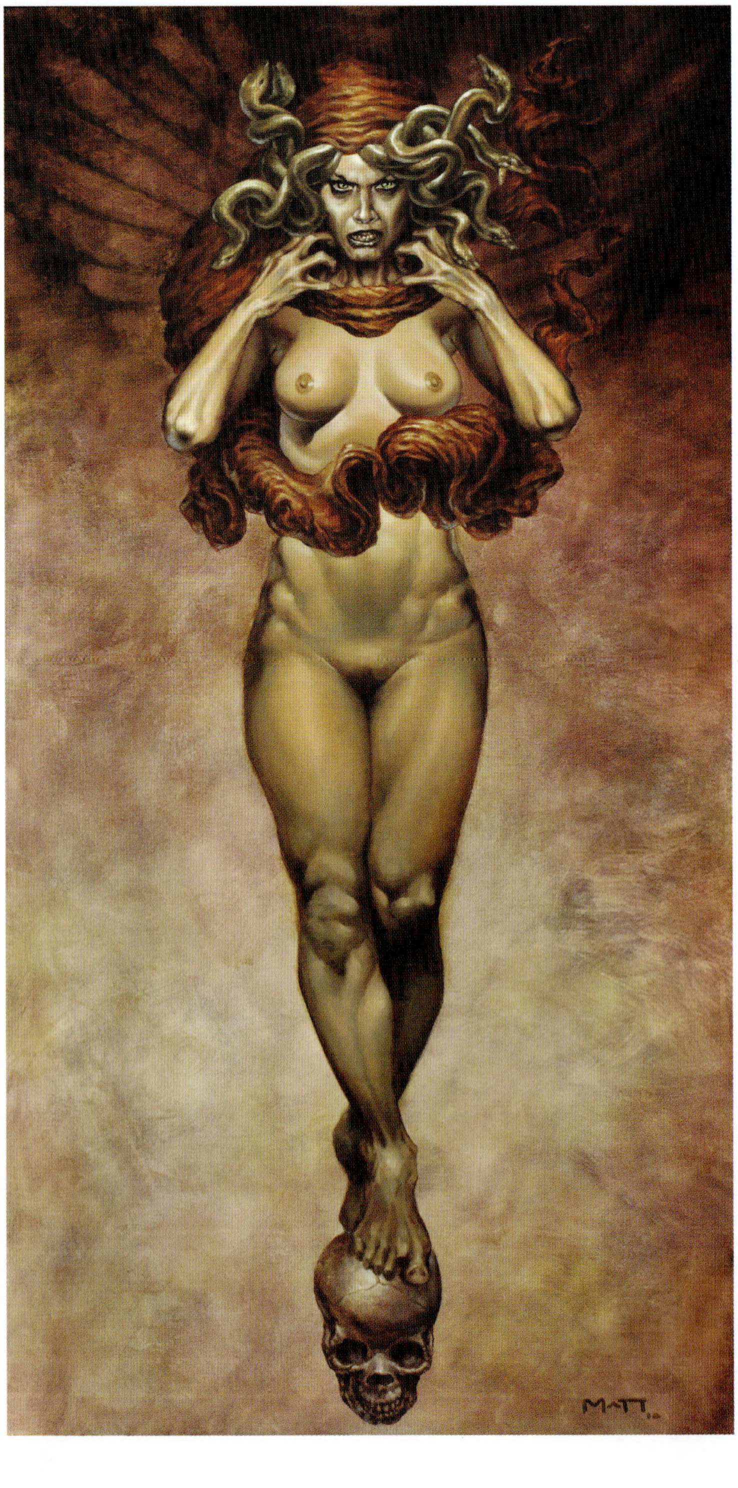

Medusa

Following Page - Zpherus Gate

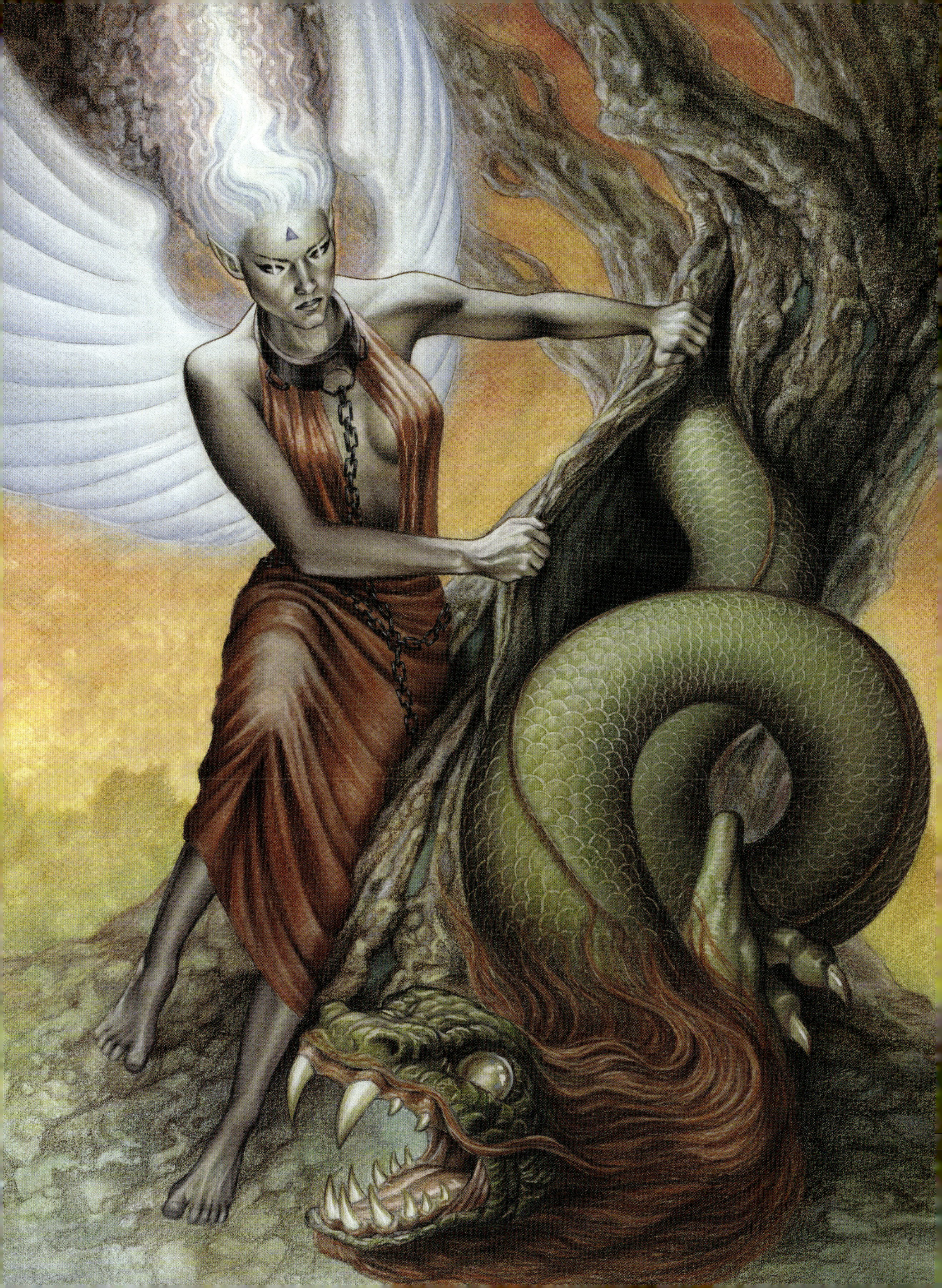

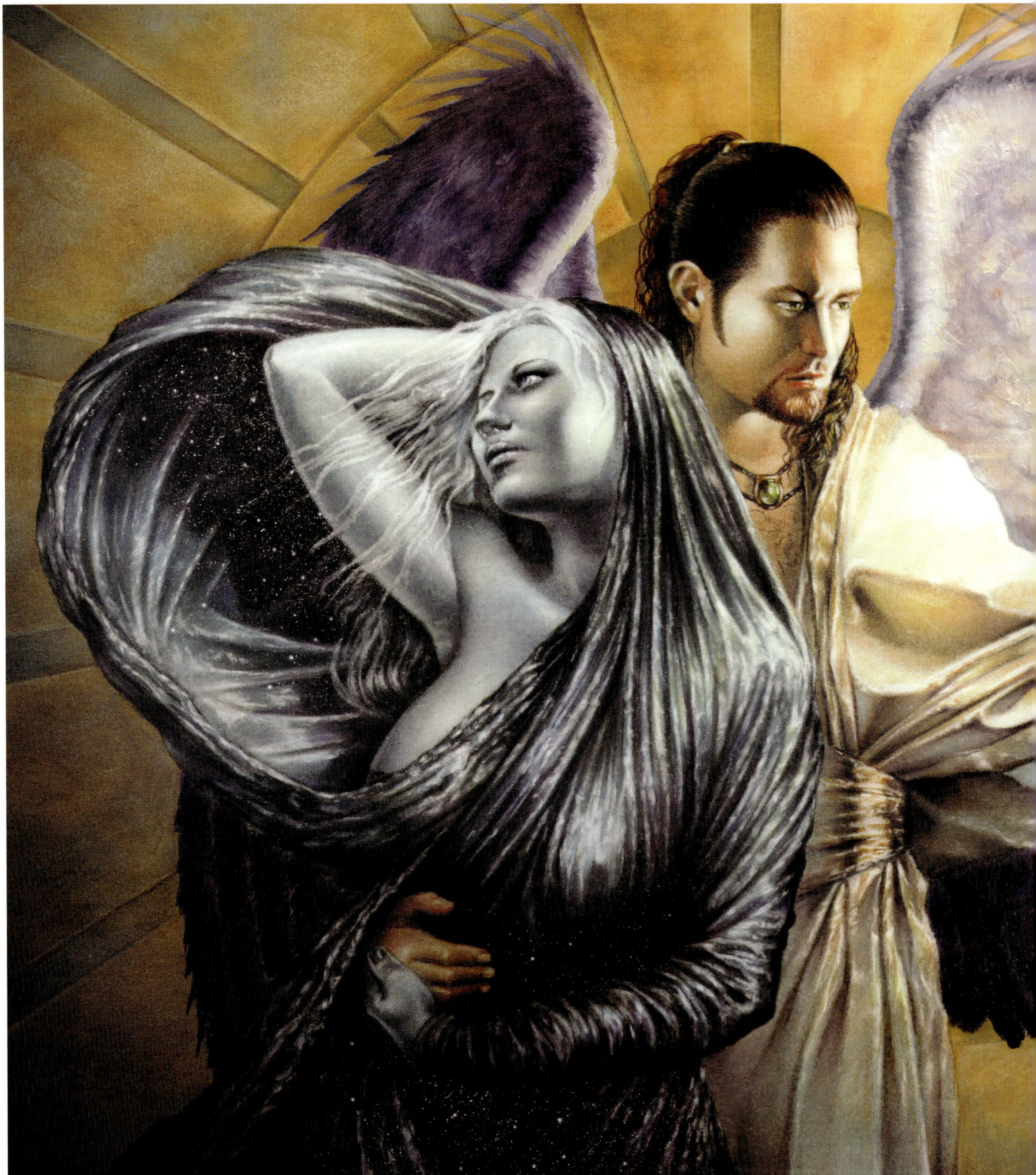

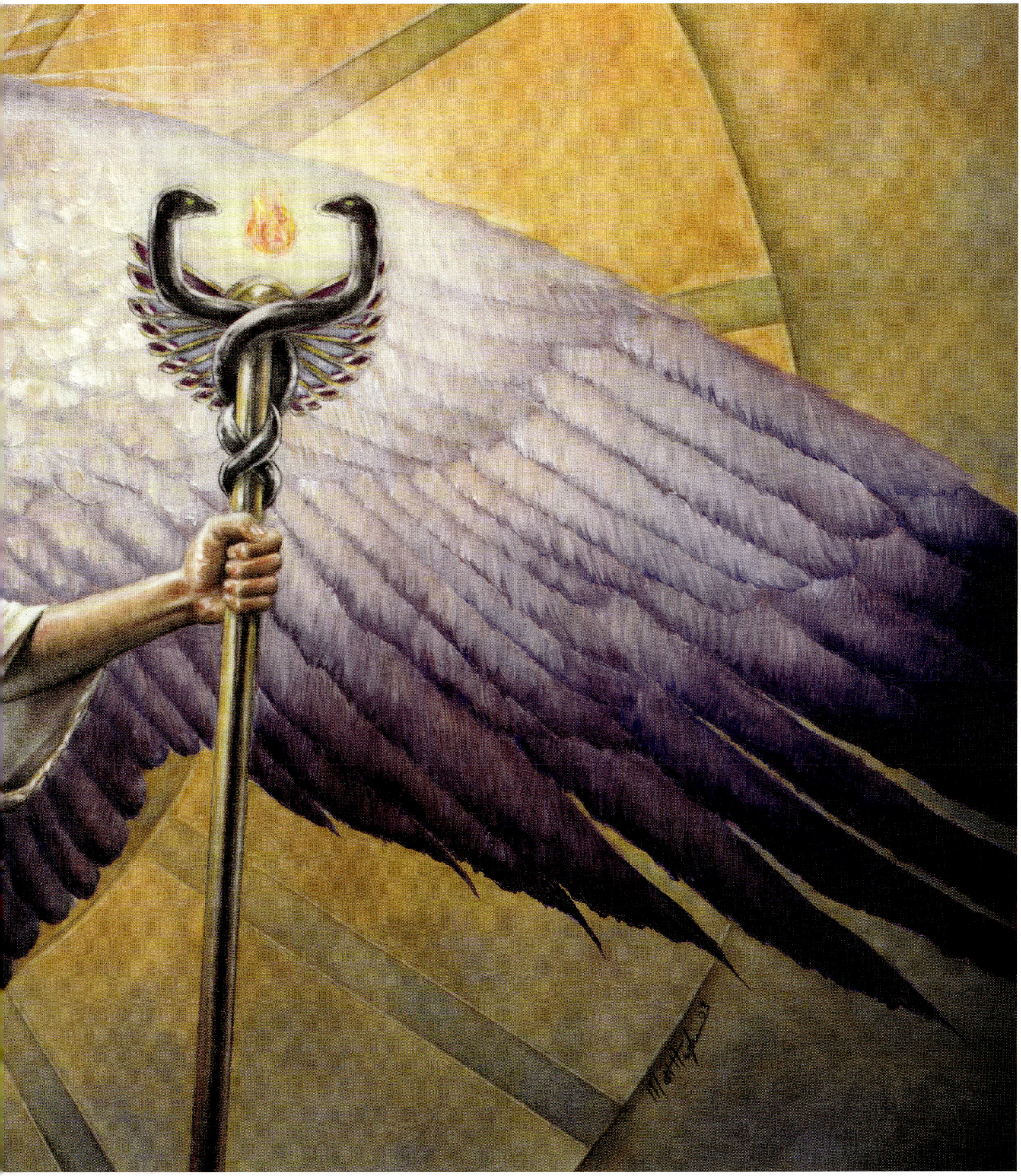

Consort of the Morning Star

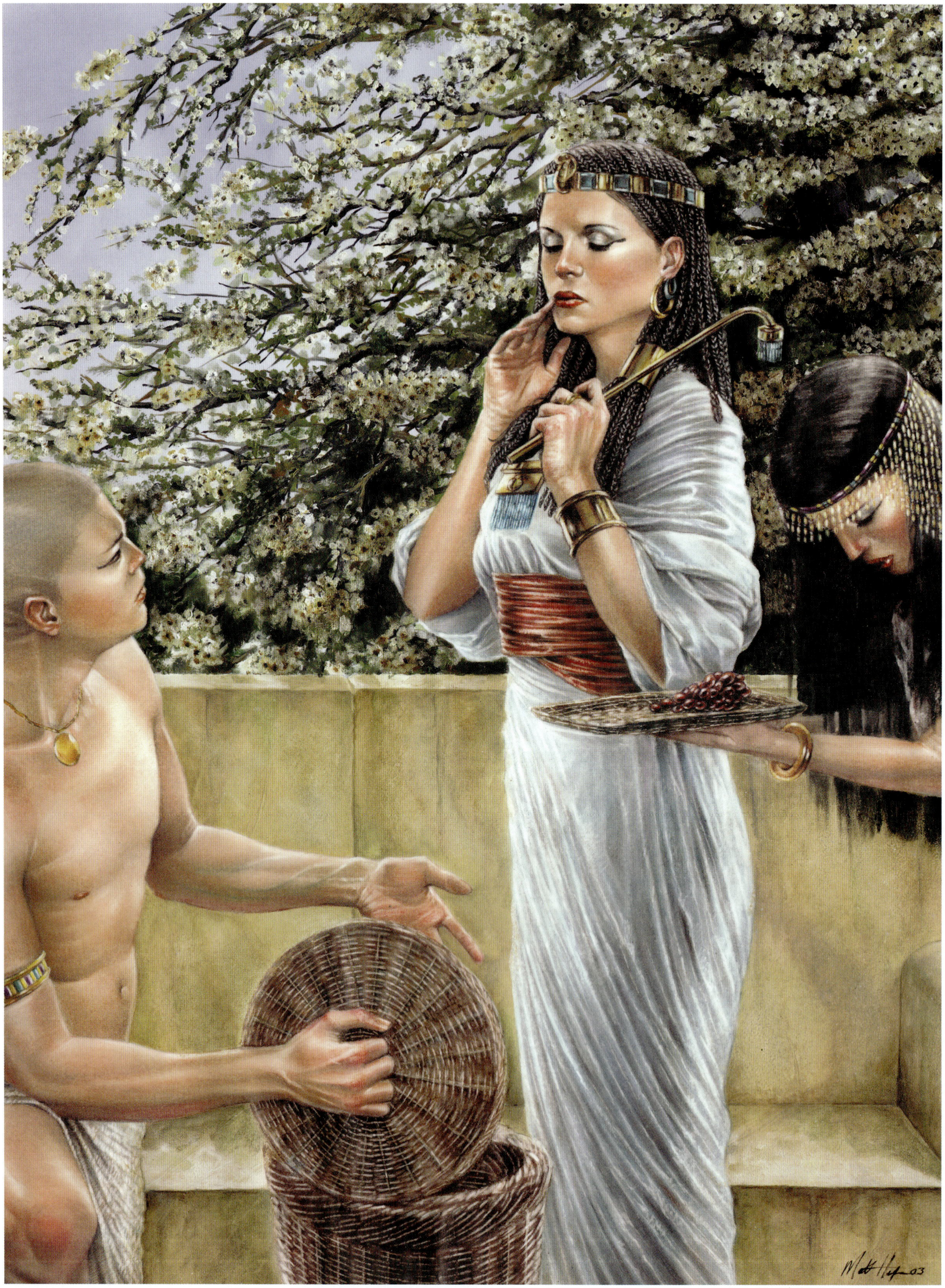

Cleopatra

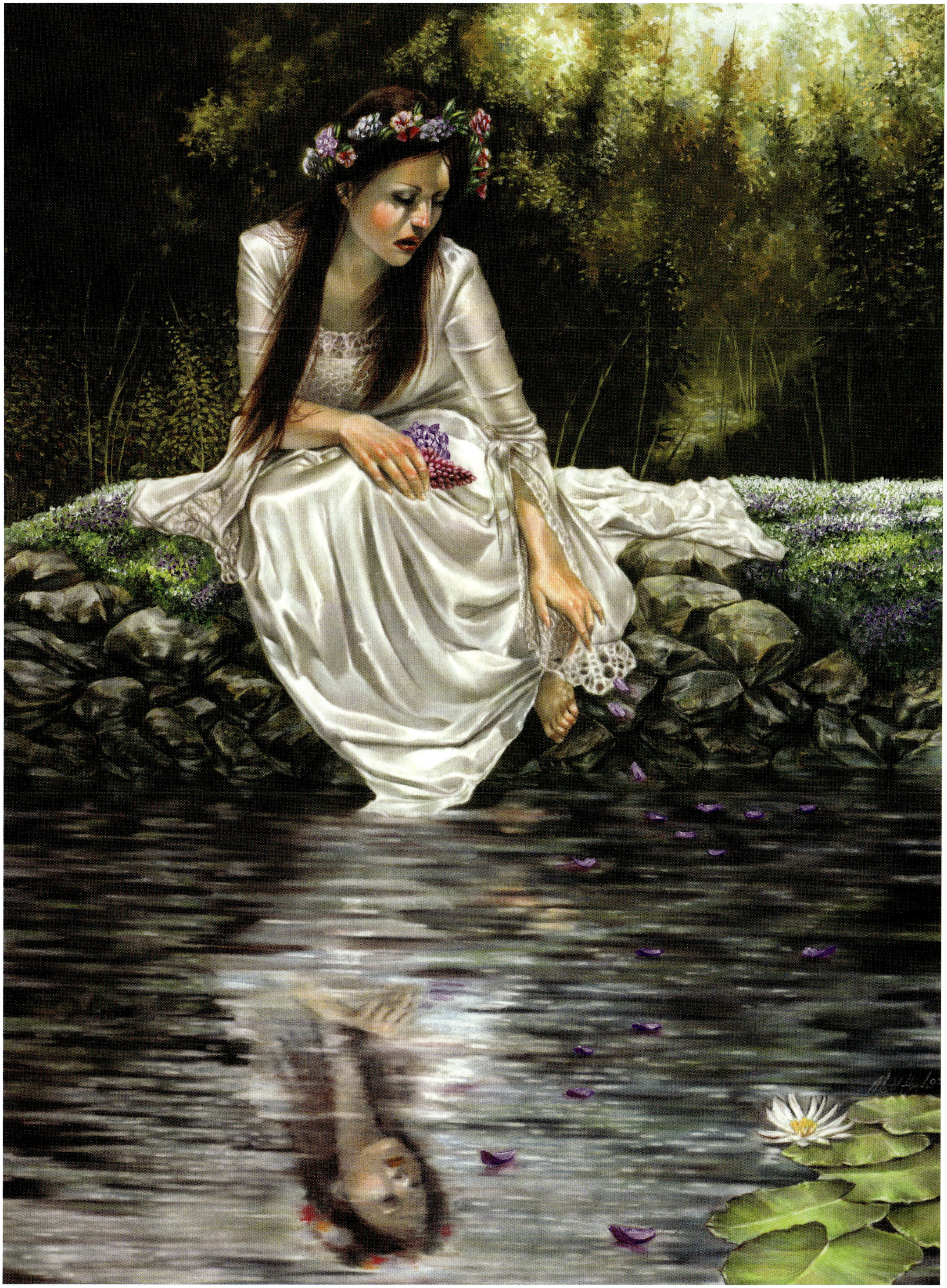

Ophelia's Lament

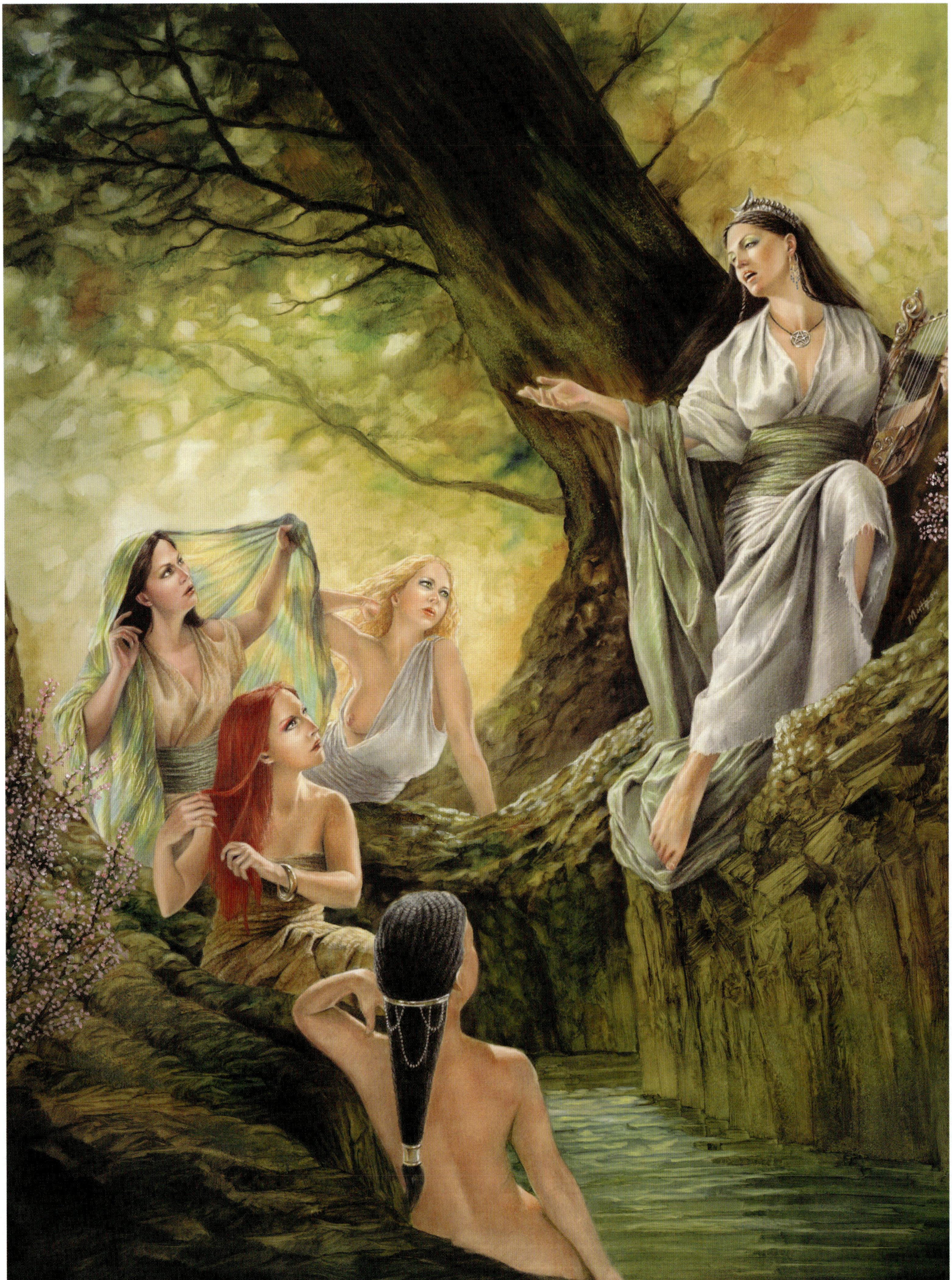

Gaia and the Elements

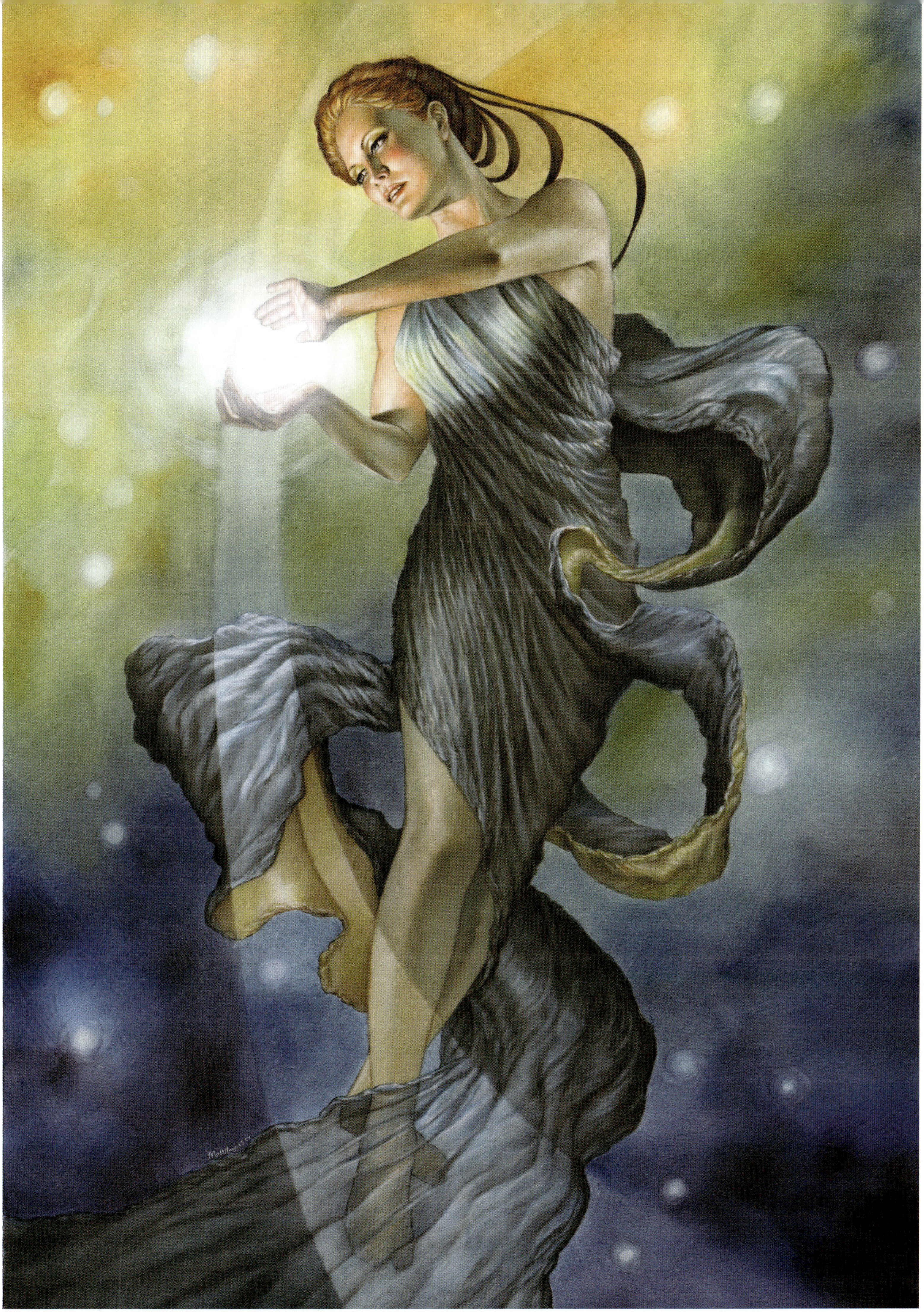

Stars

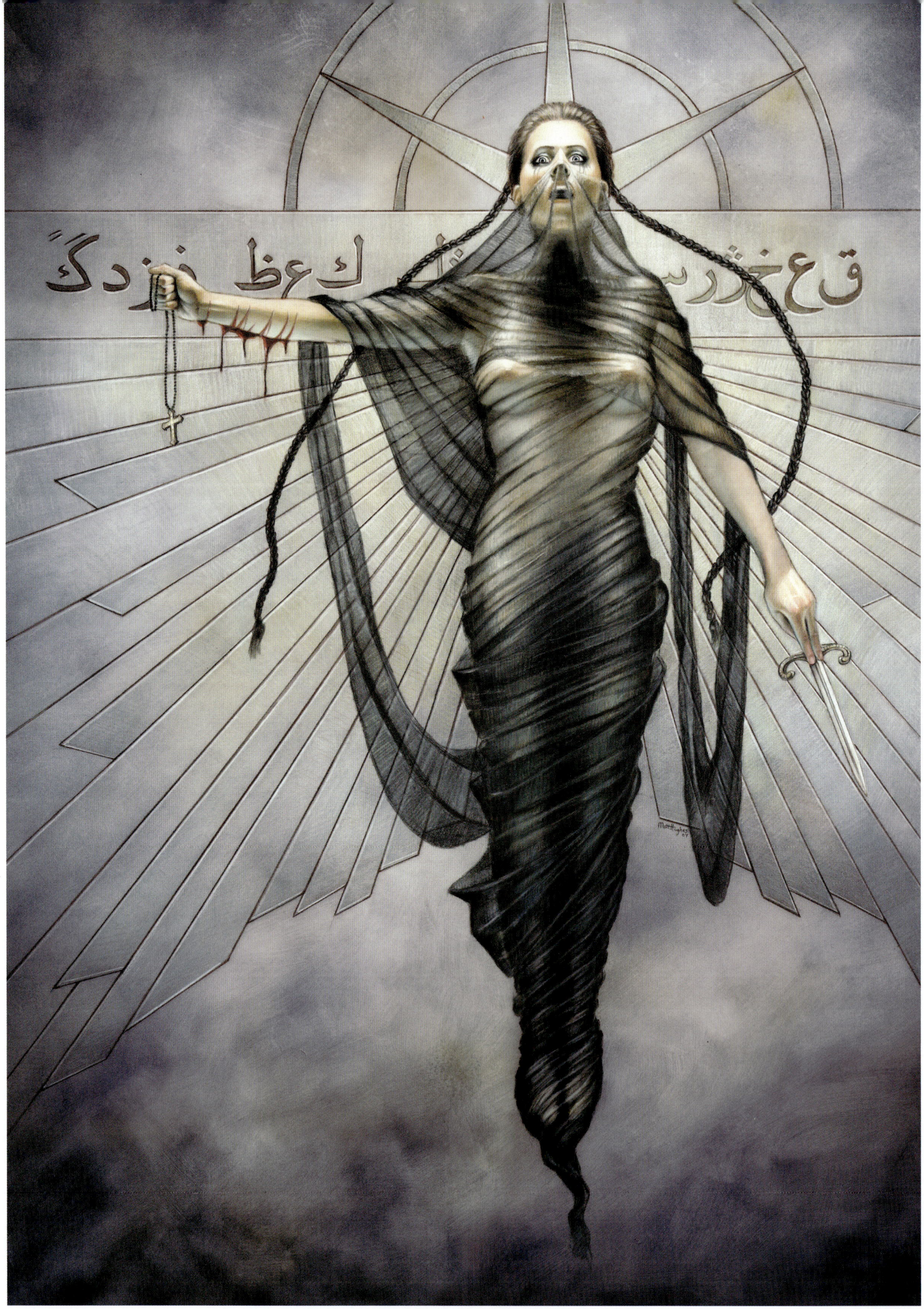

Judge Not Thy Neighbor

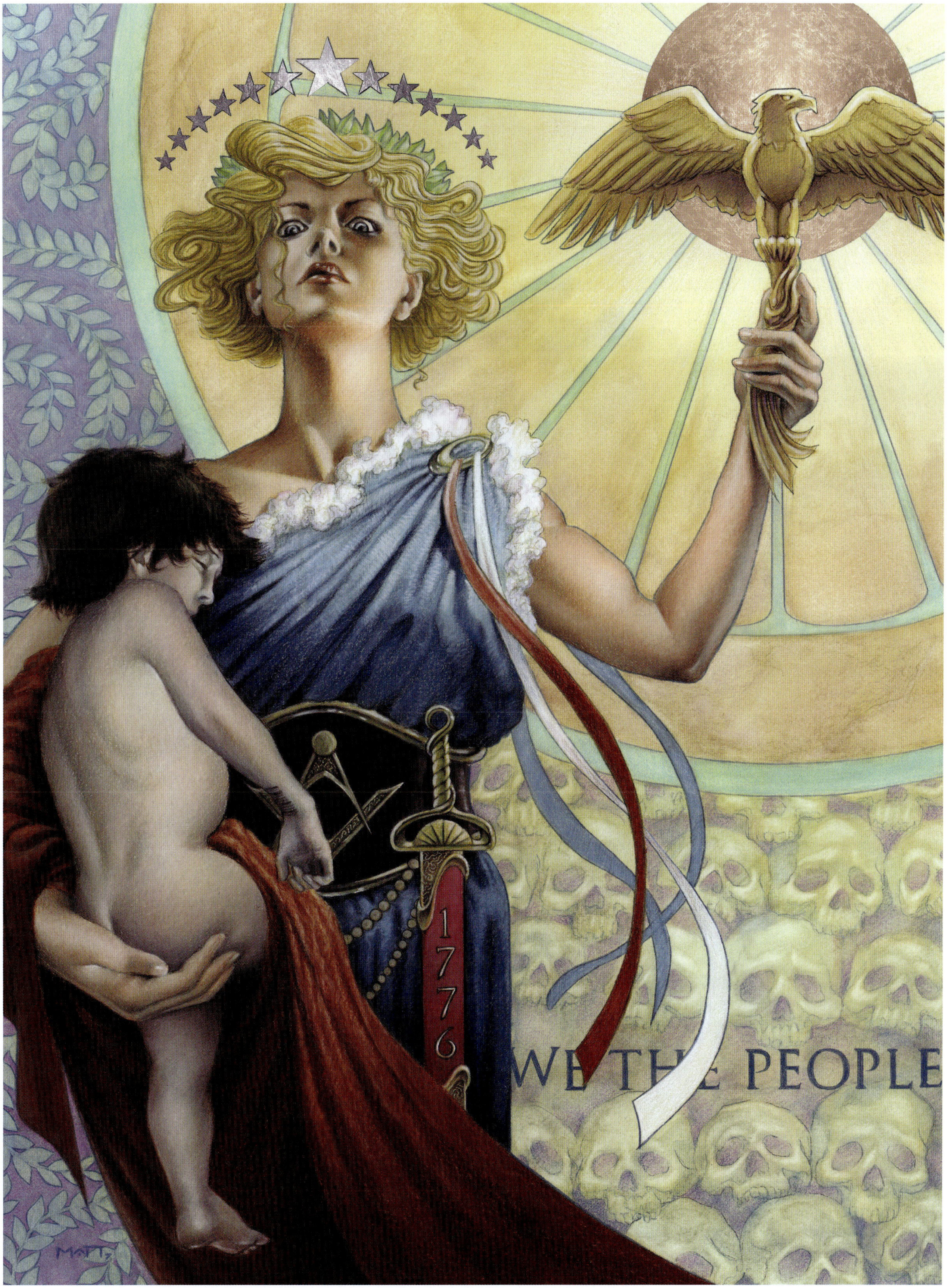

Liberty

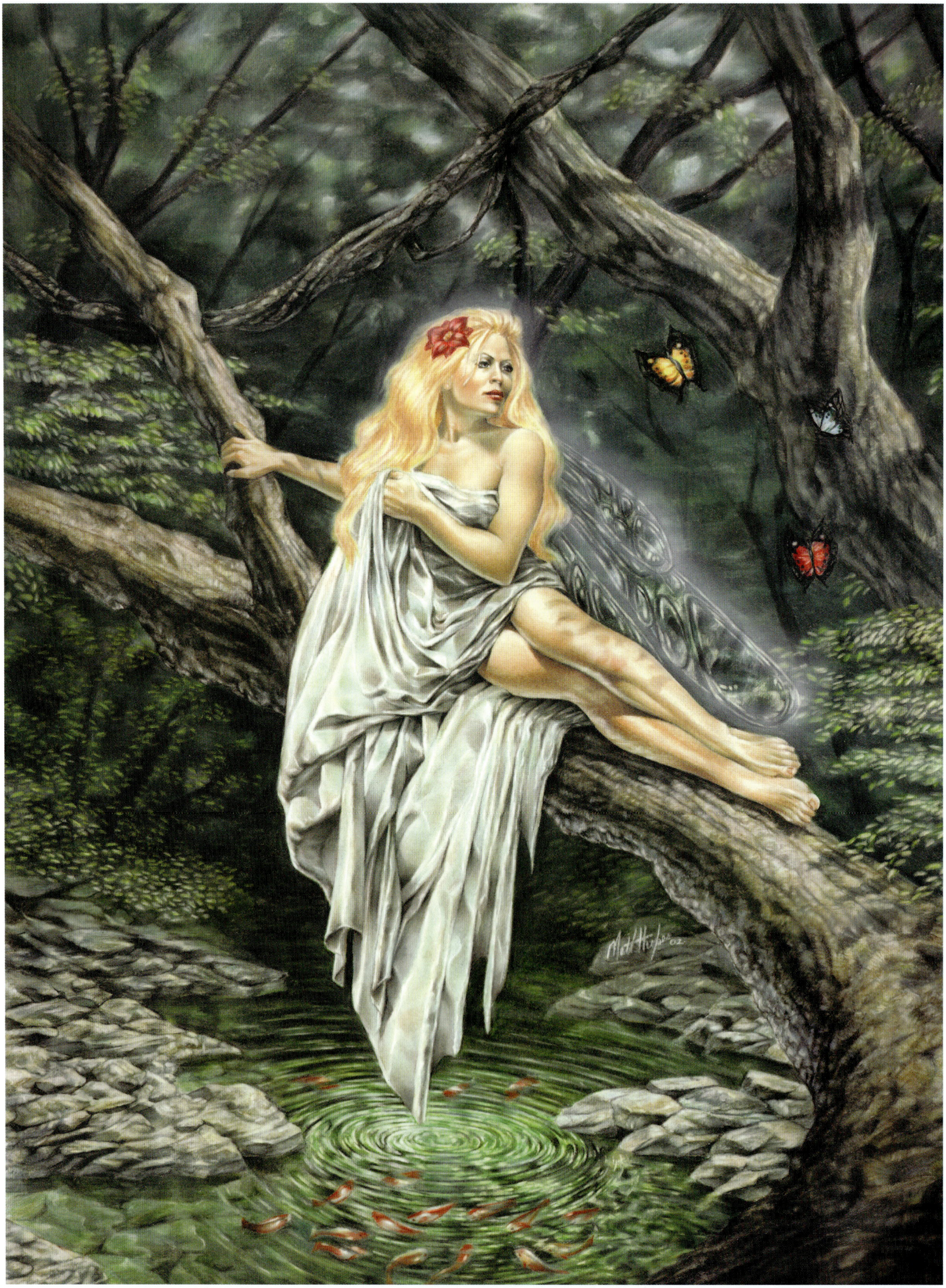

Dryad

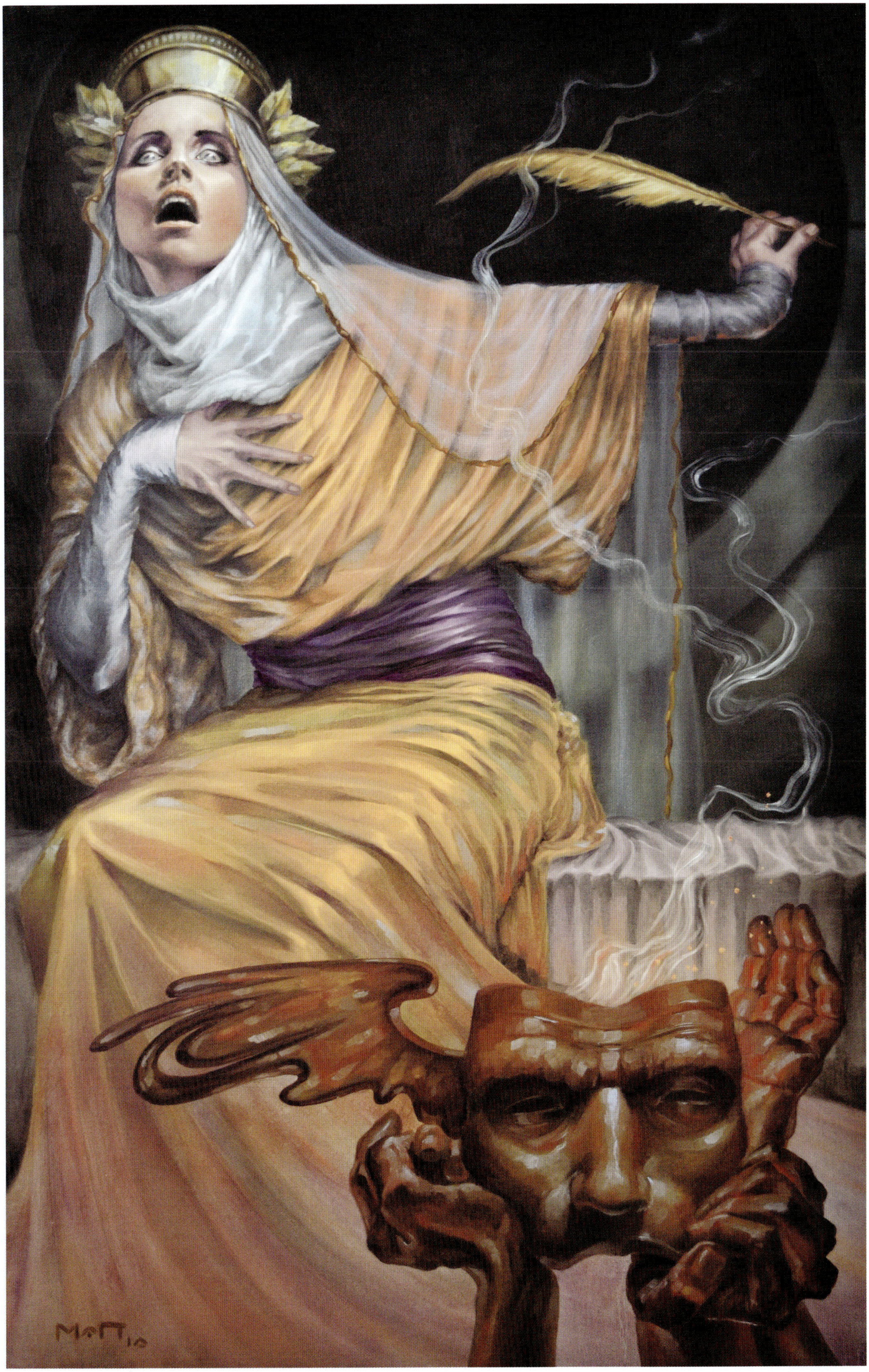

The Oracle

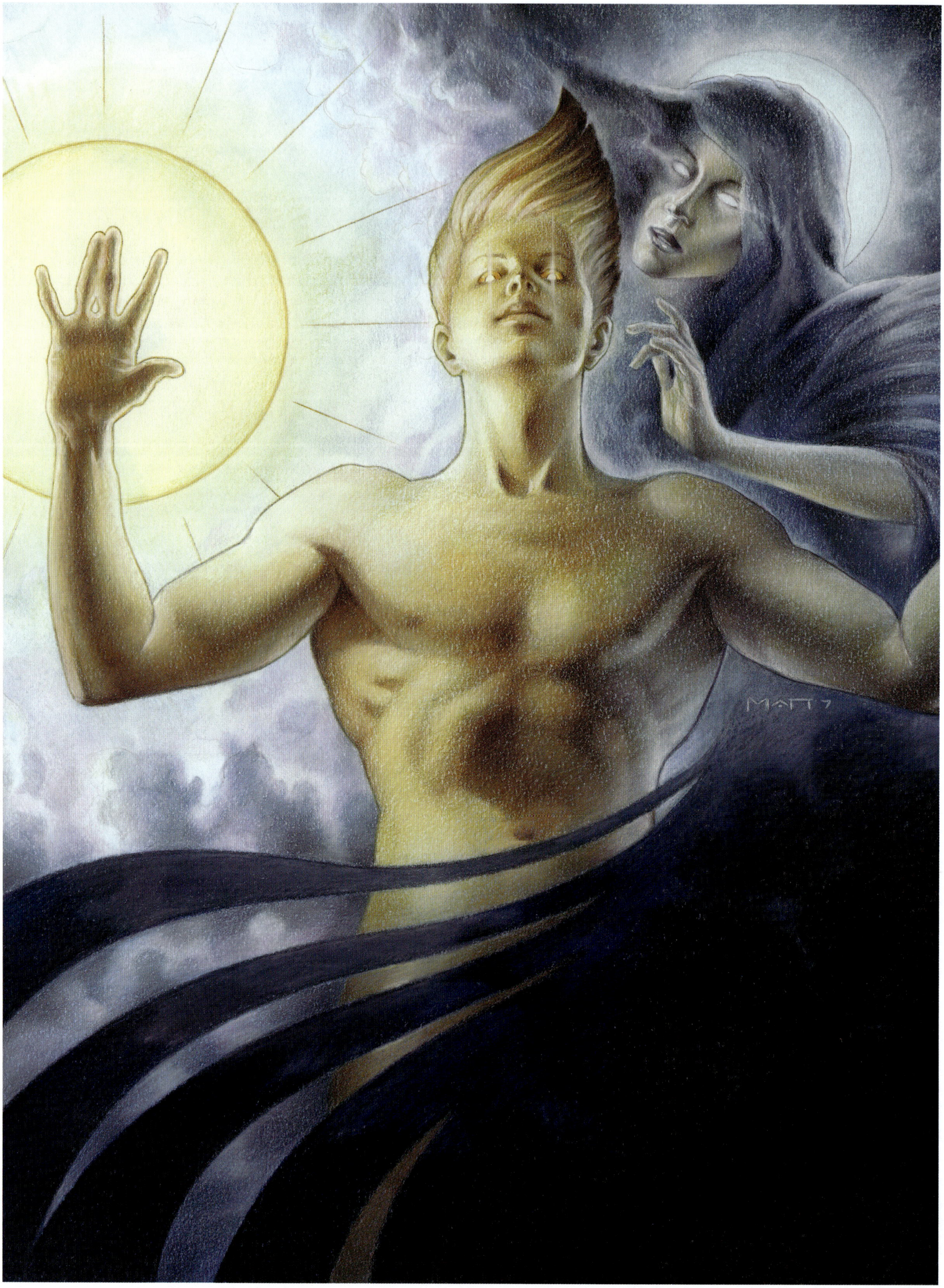

Sun

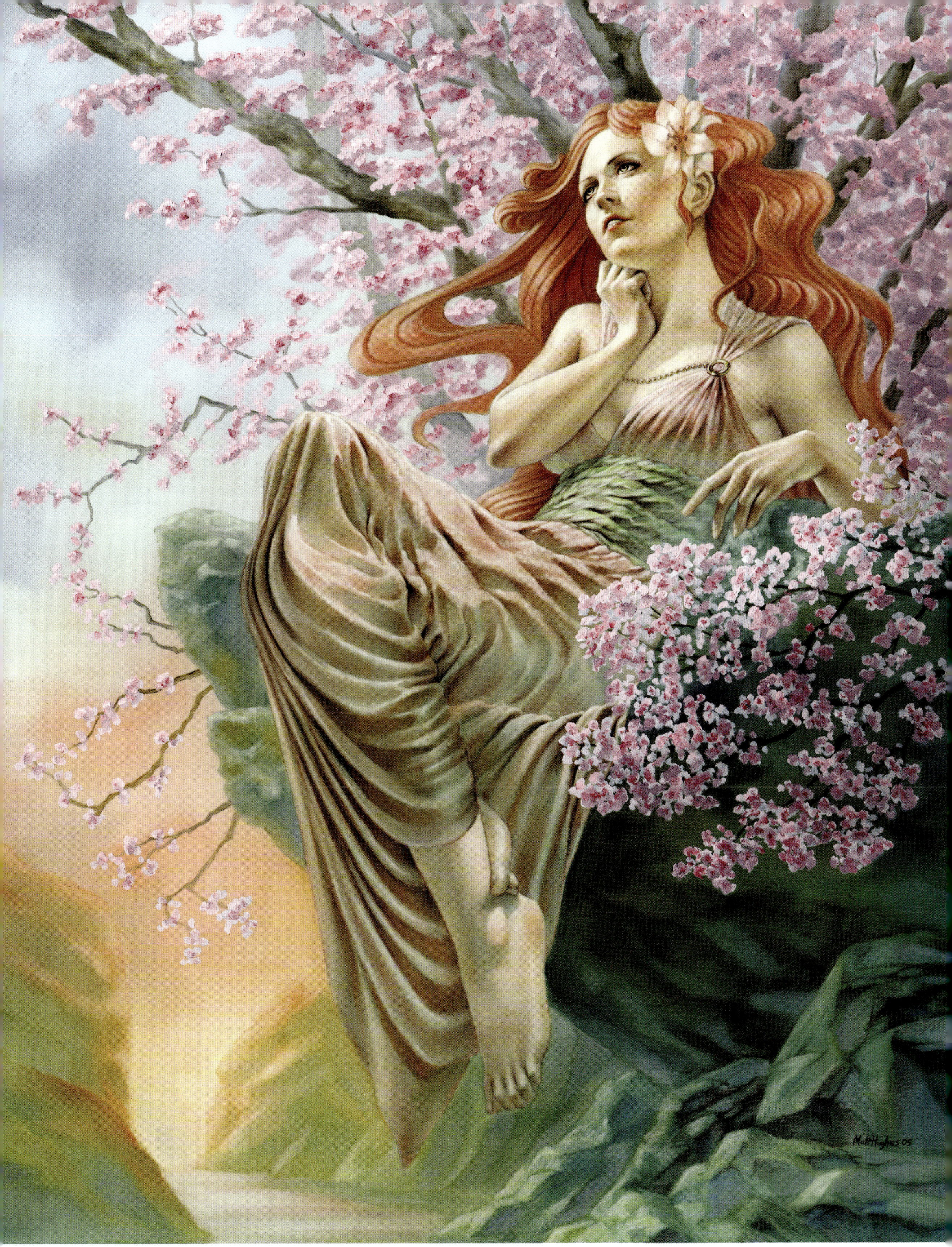

Contemplation of Summer

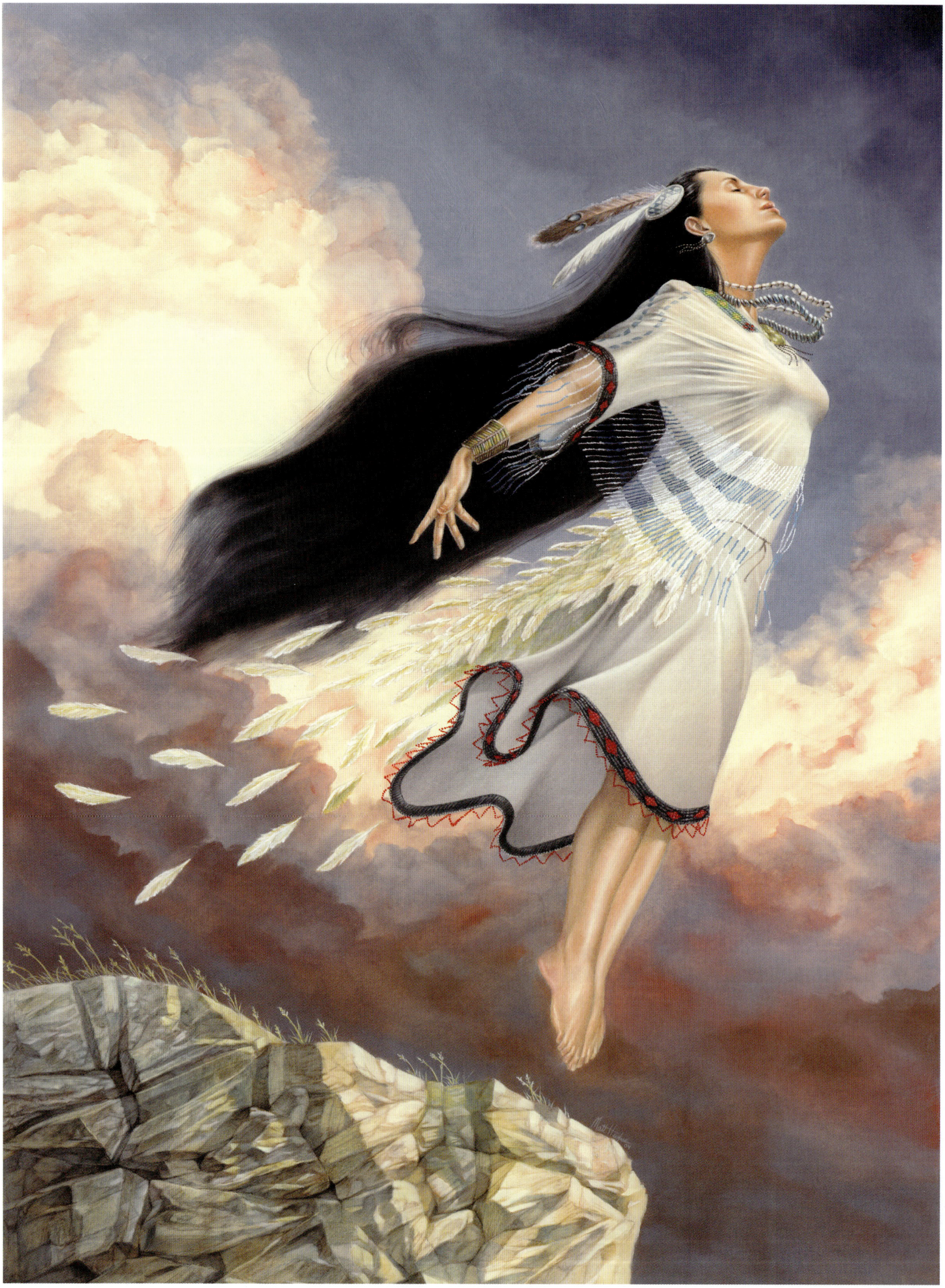

Spirit of the Wind

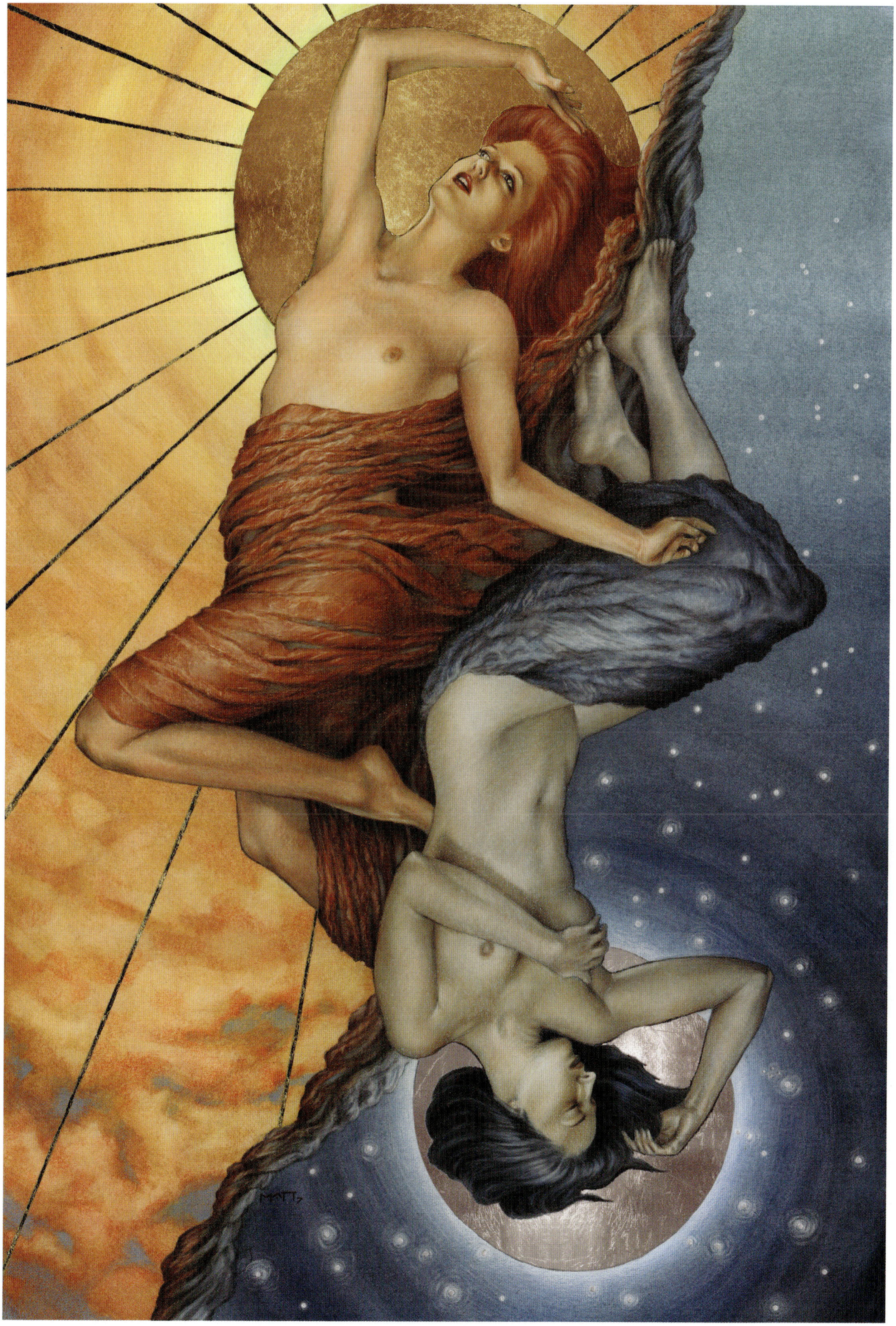

Sun/Moon

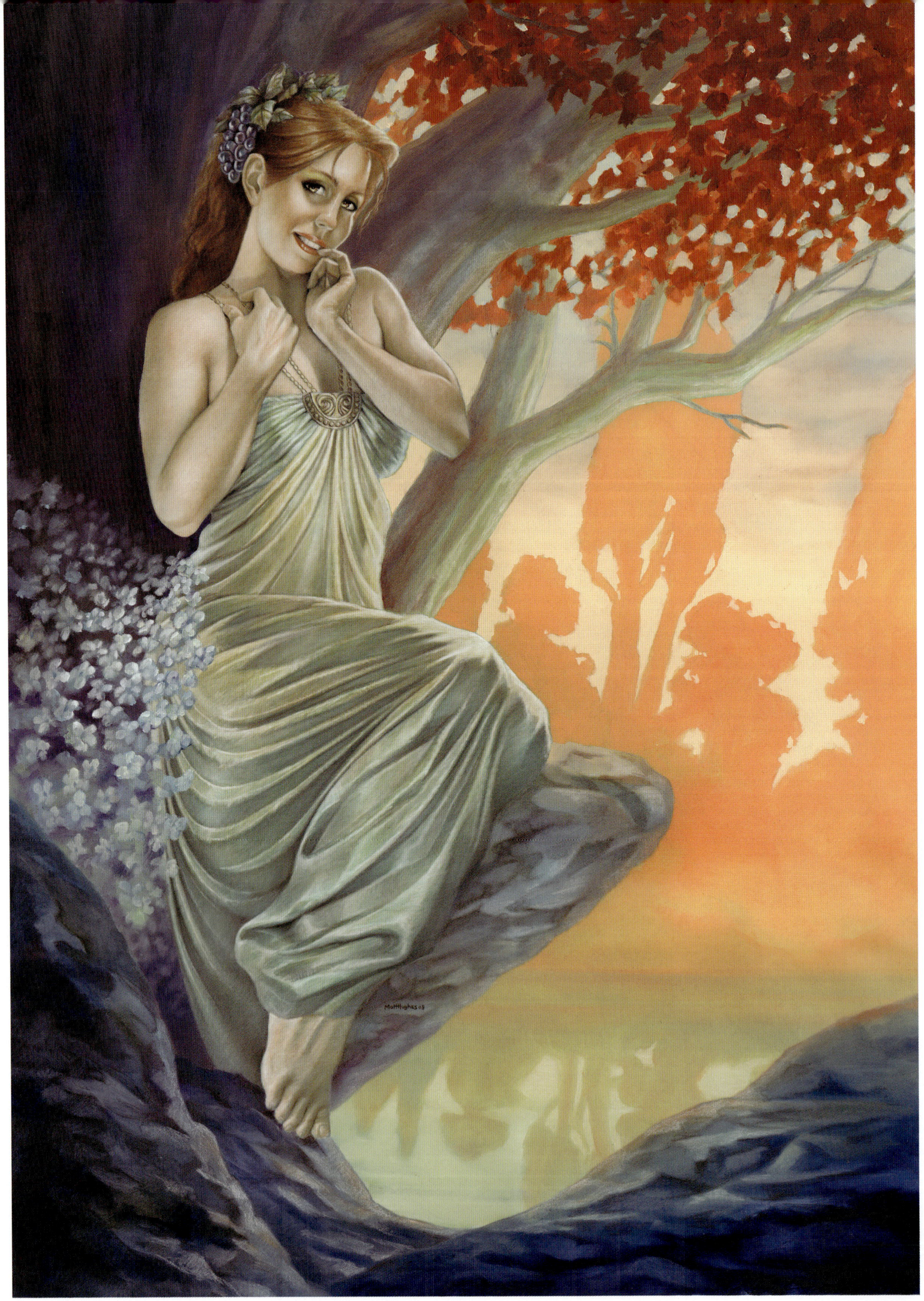

Fall

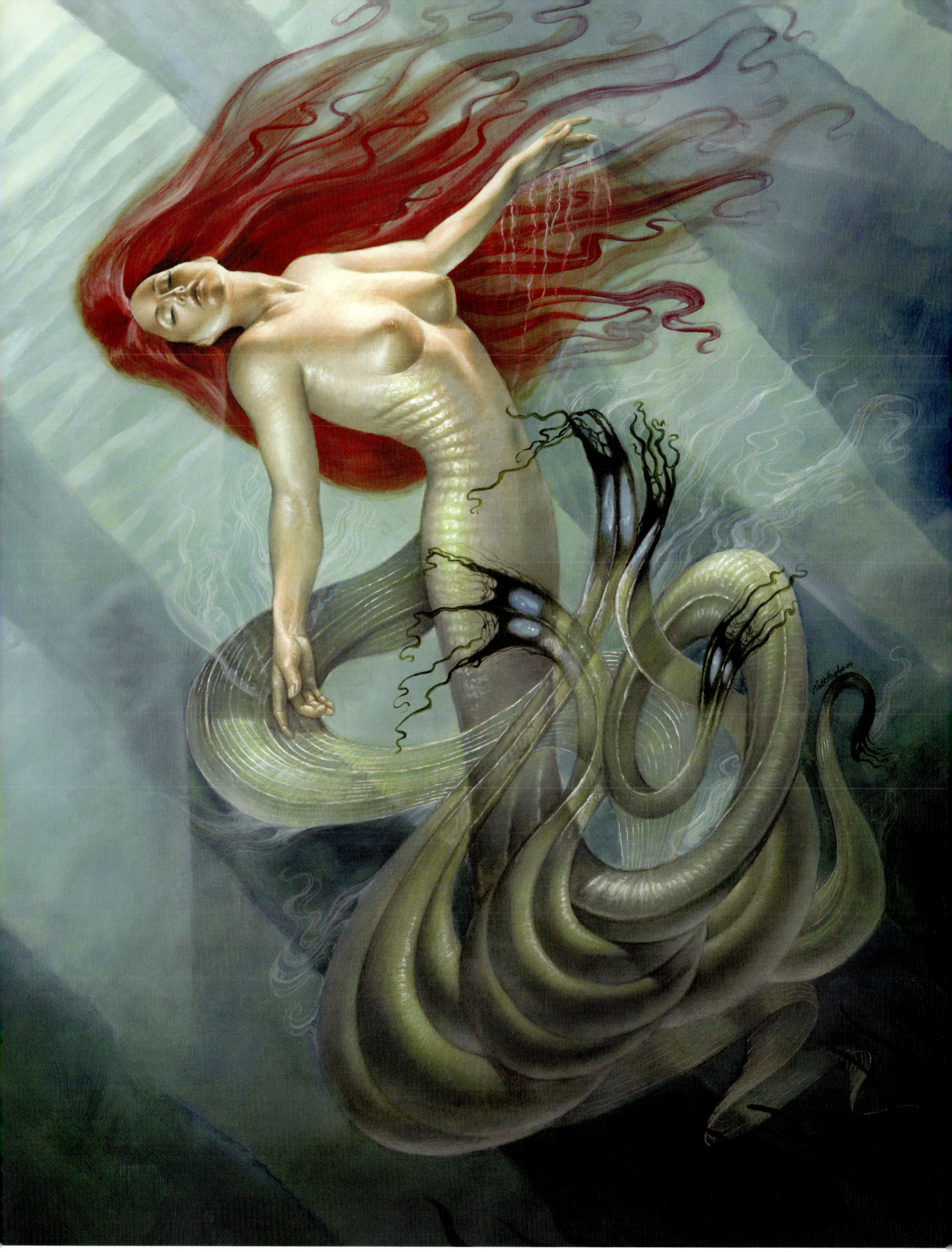

Ocean's Ecstasy

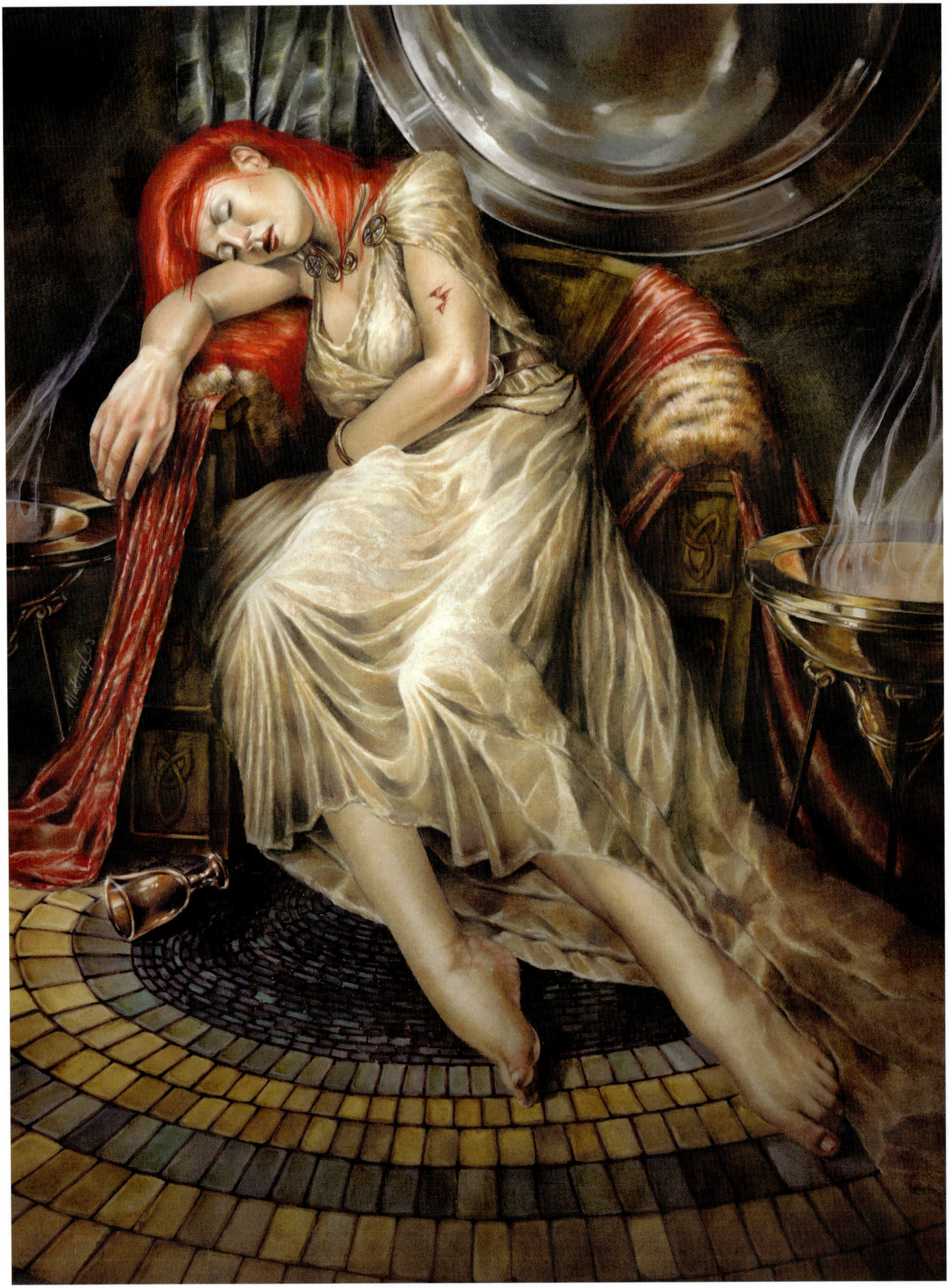

Death of the Inceni Queen

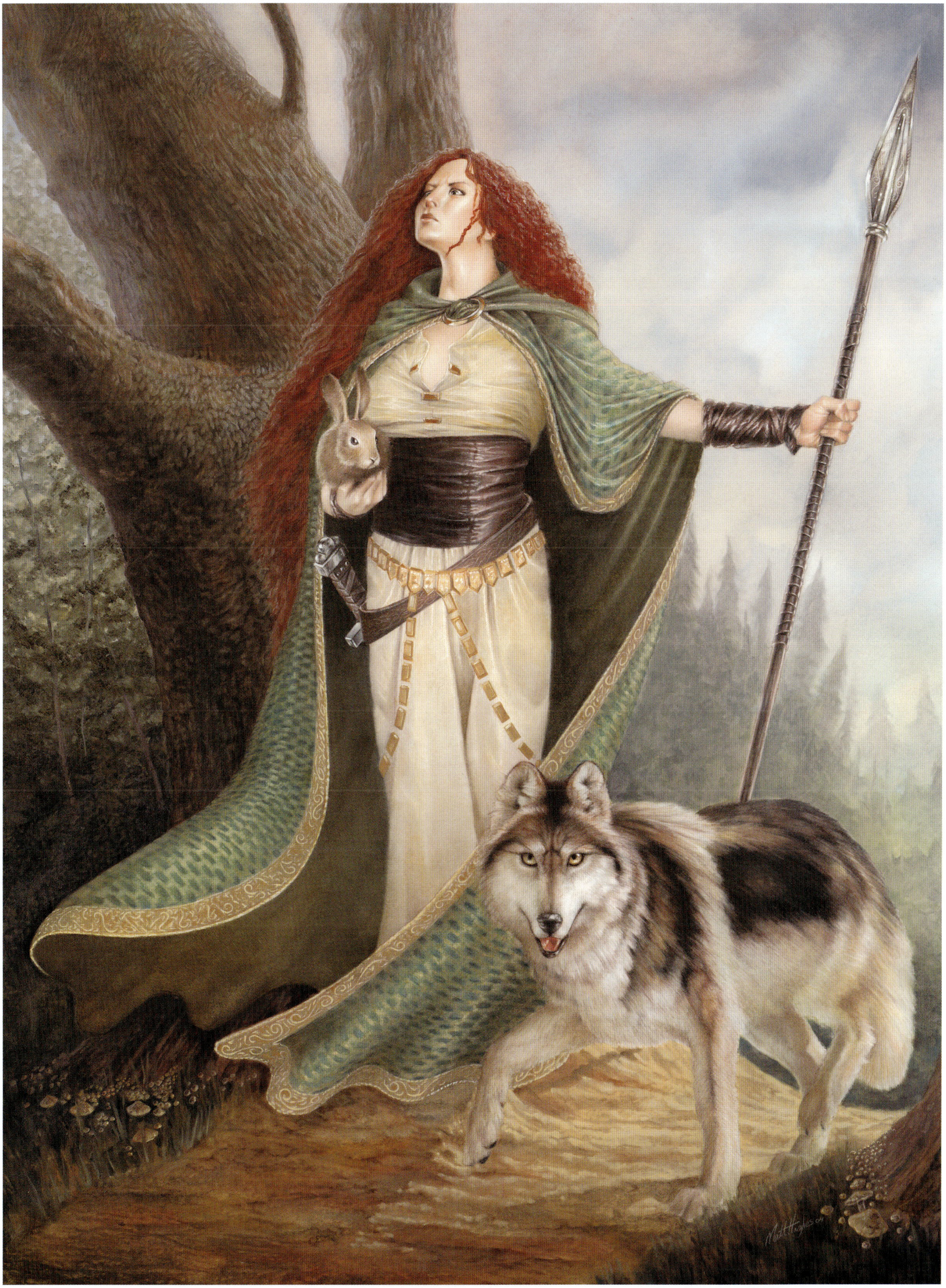

Queen Boudicca

Spring

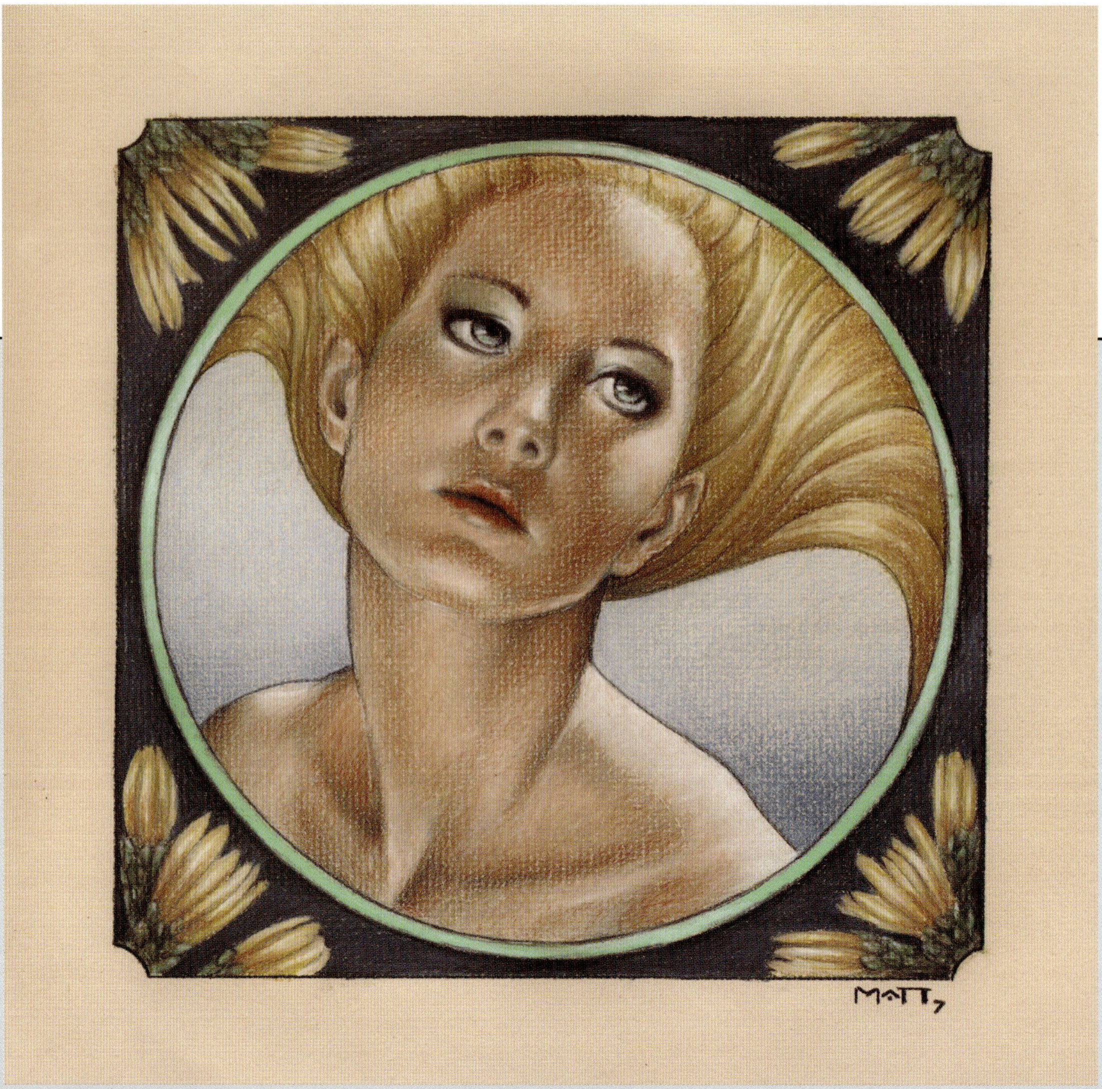

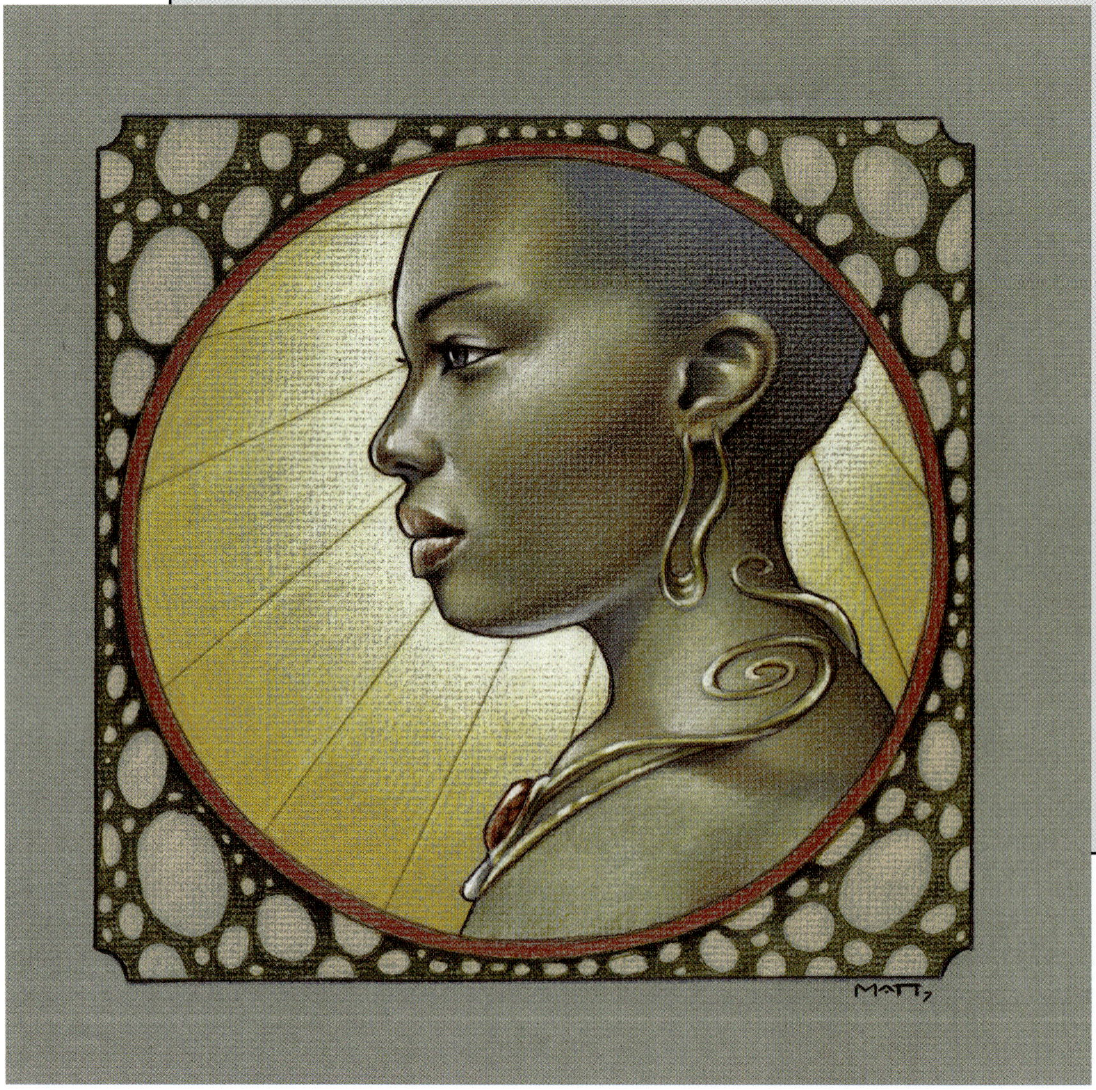

Summer

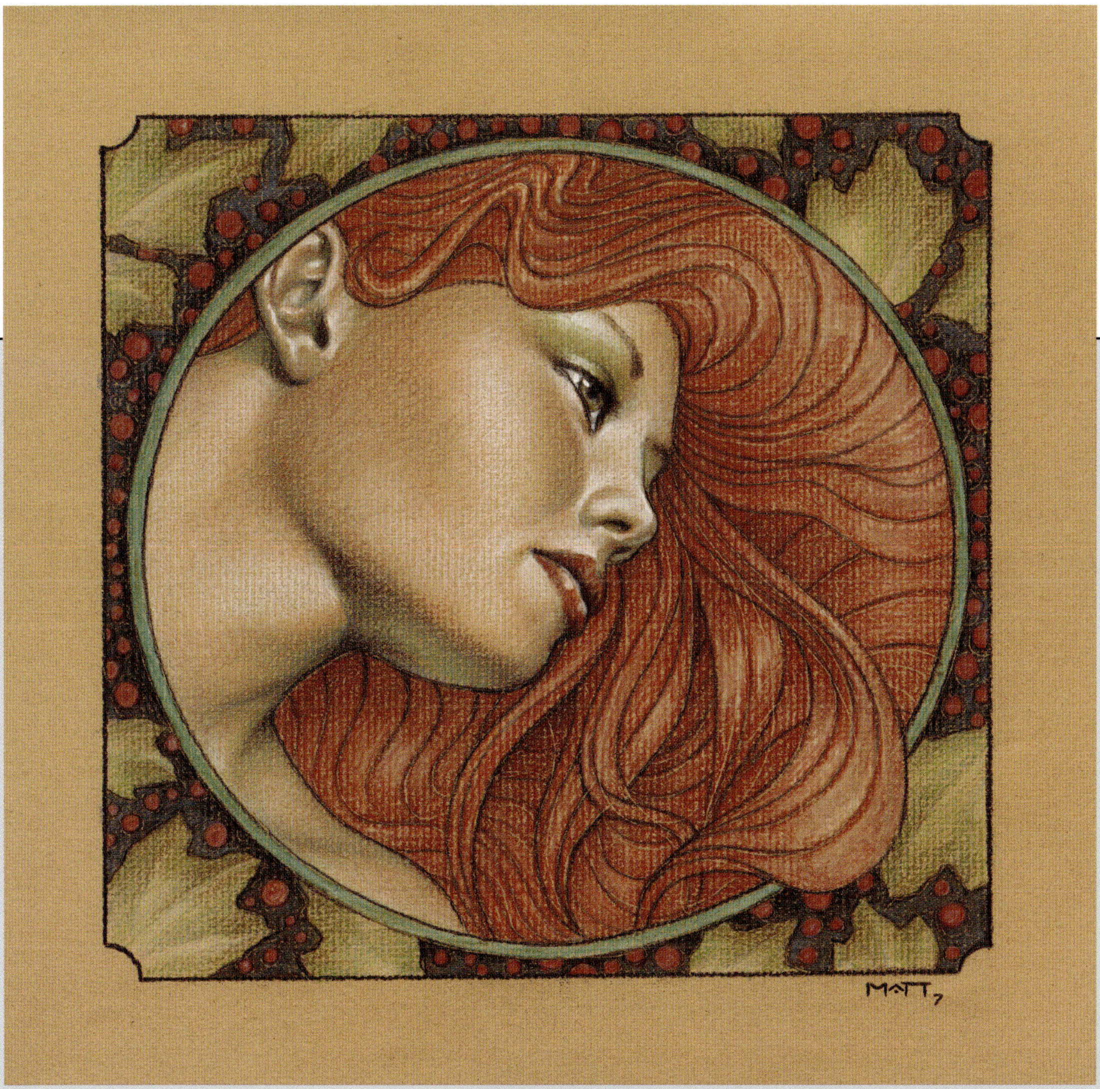

Fall

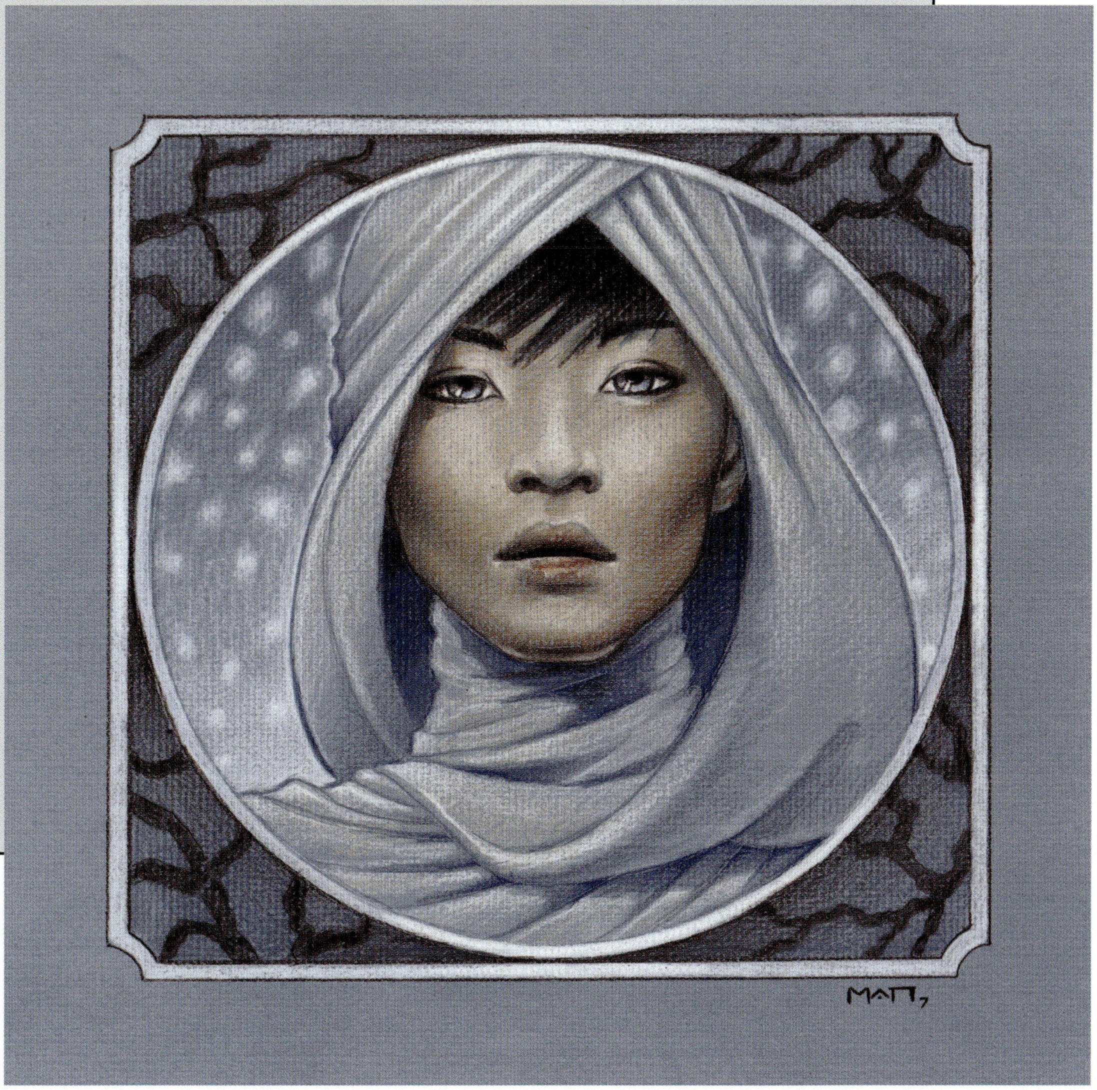

Winter

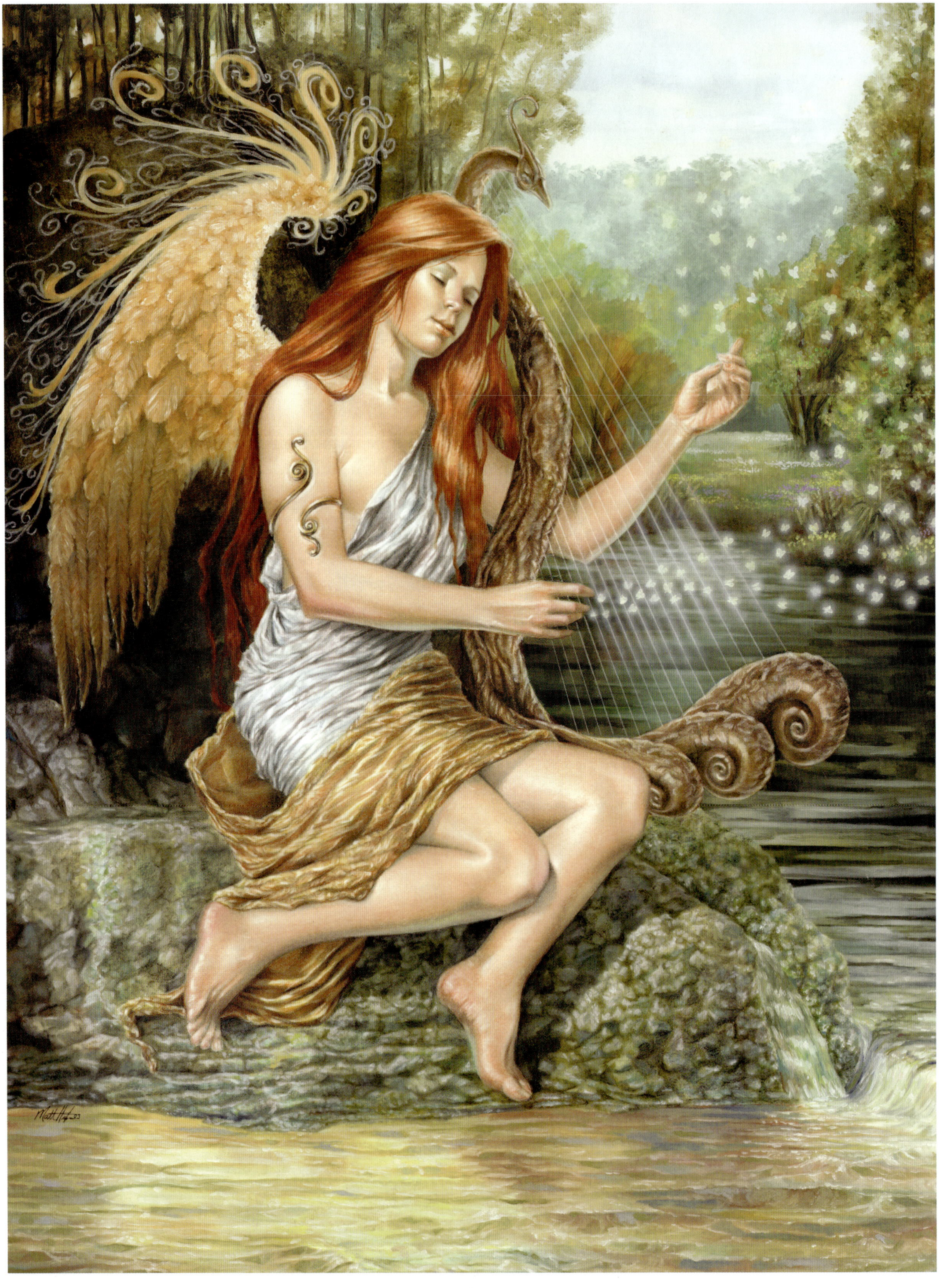

Spring

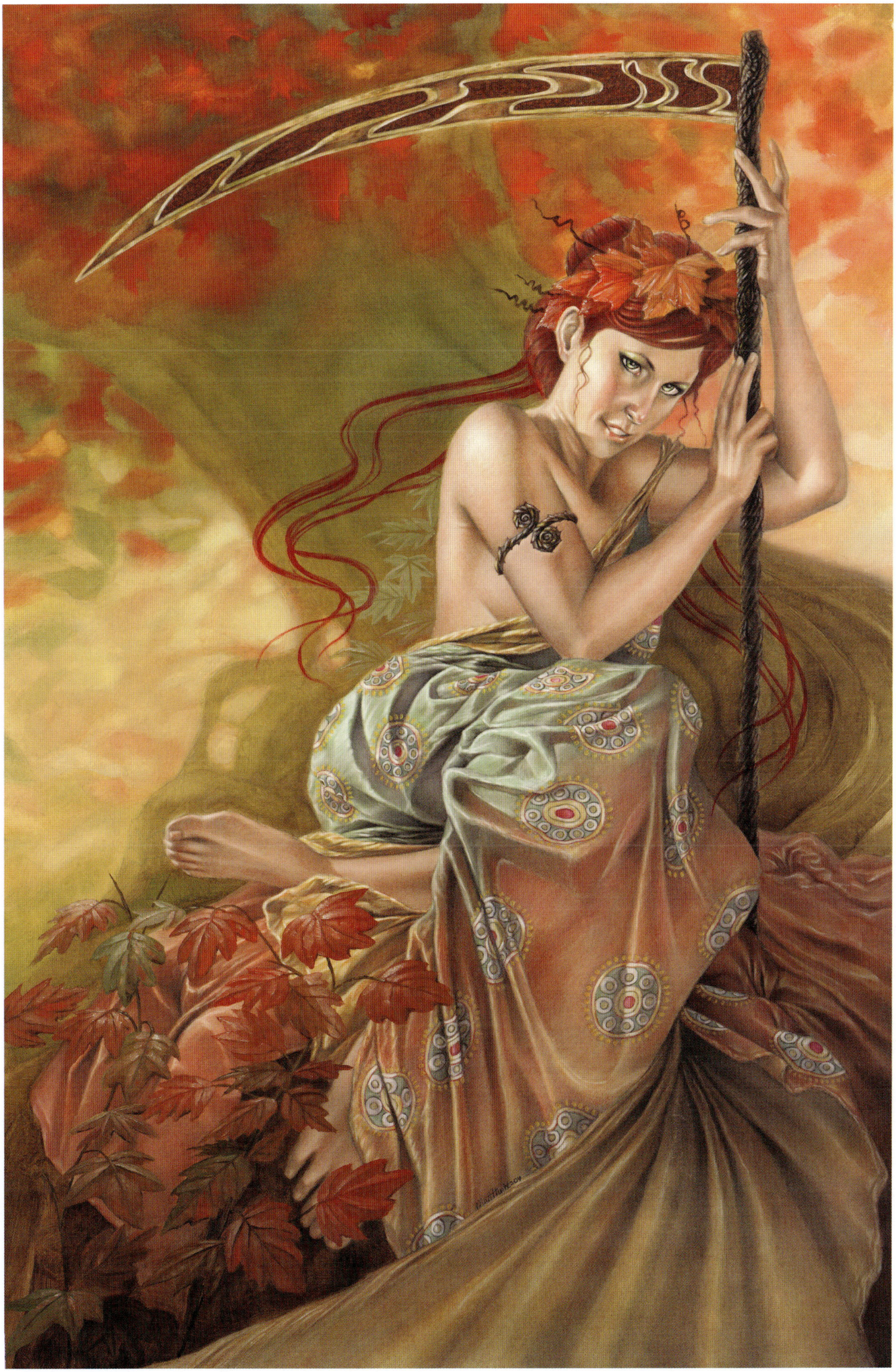

Autumnal

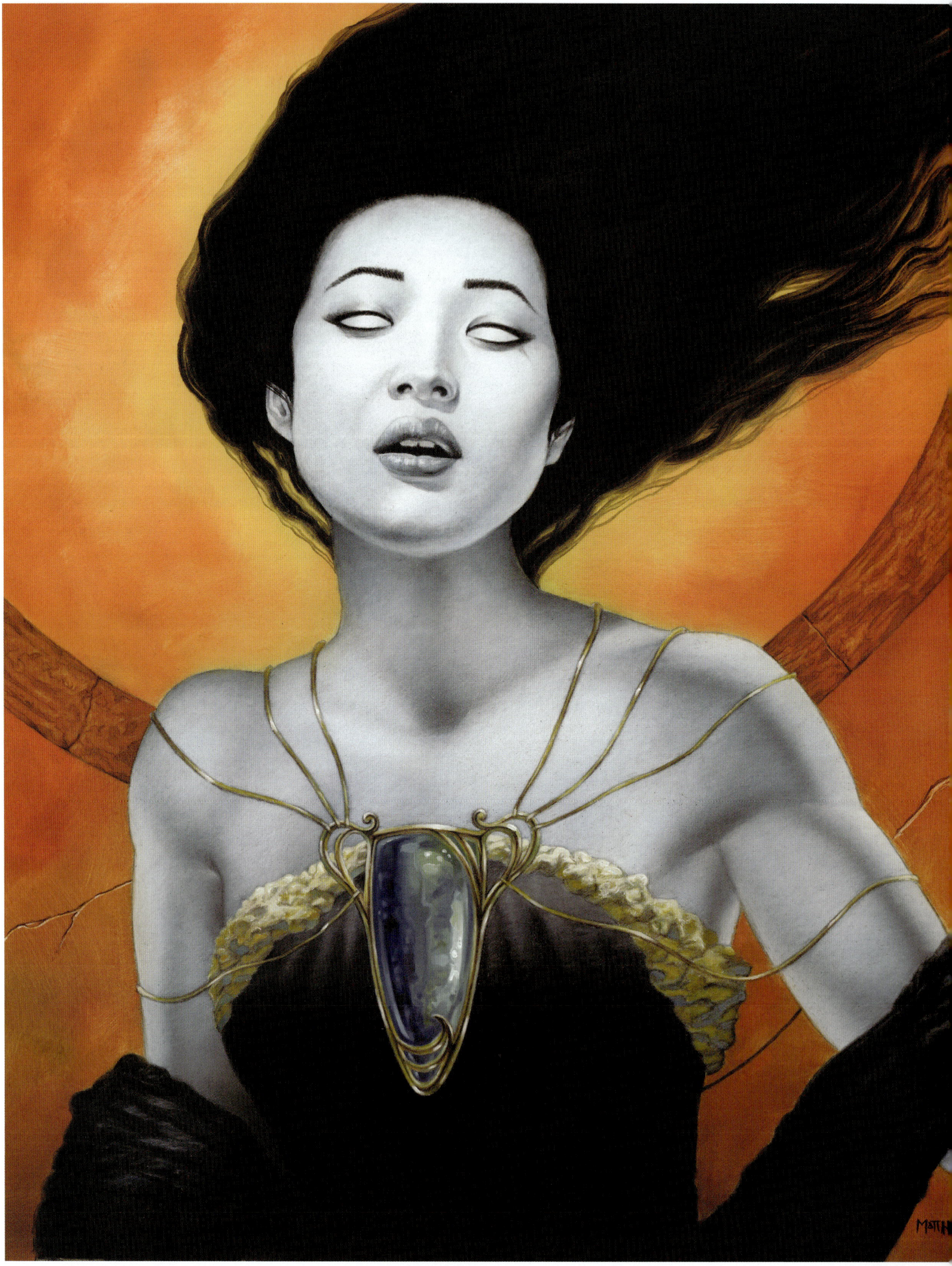

Circle

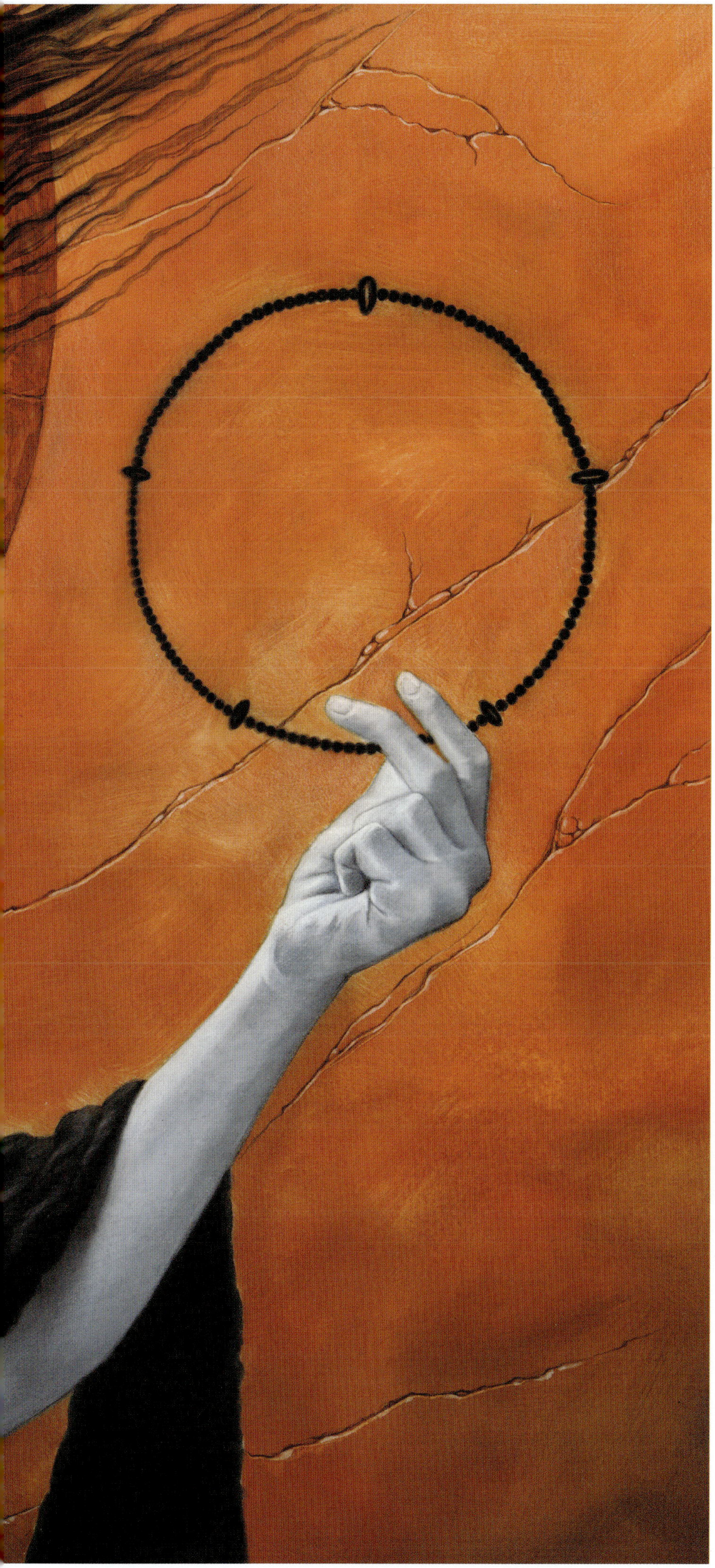

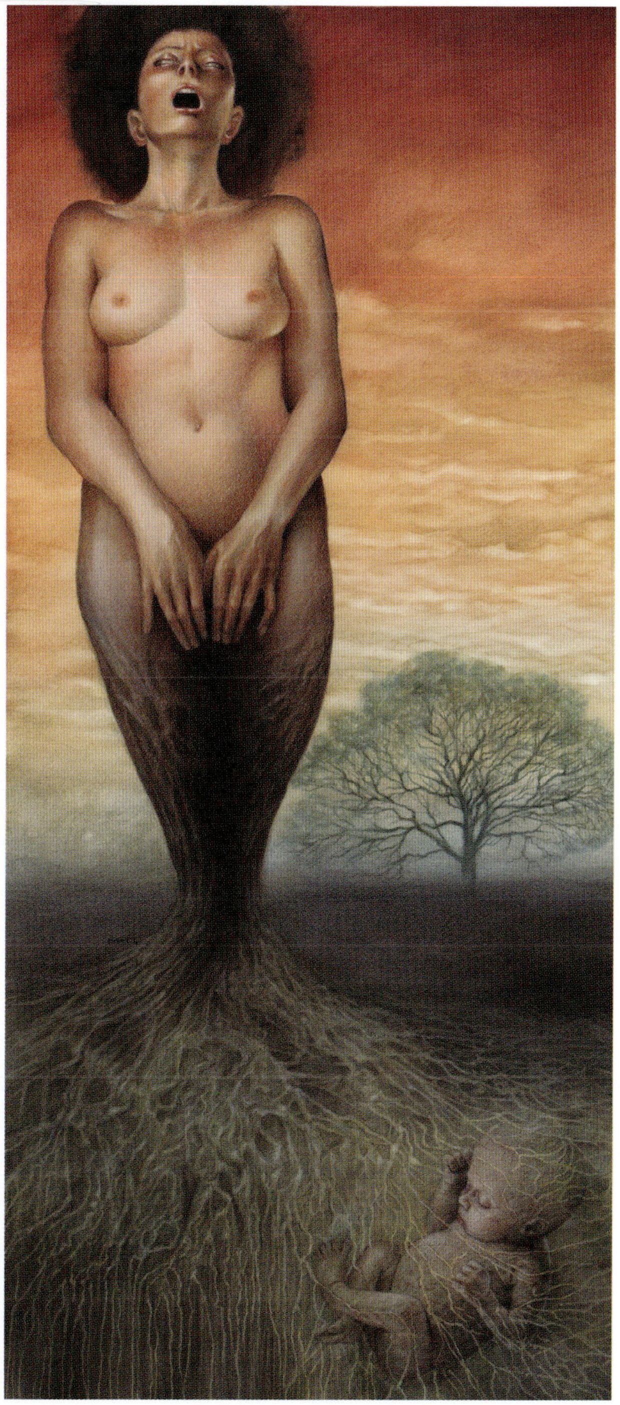

Love of Mother

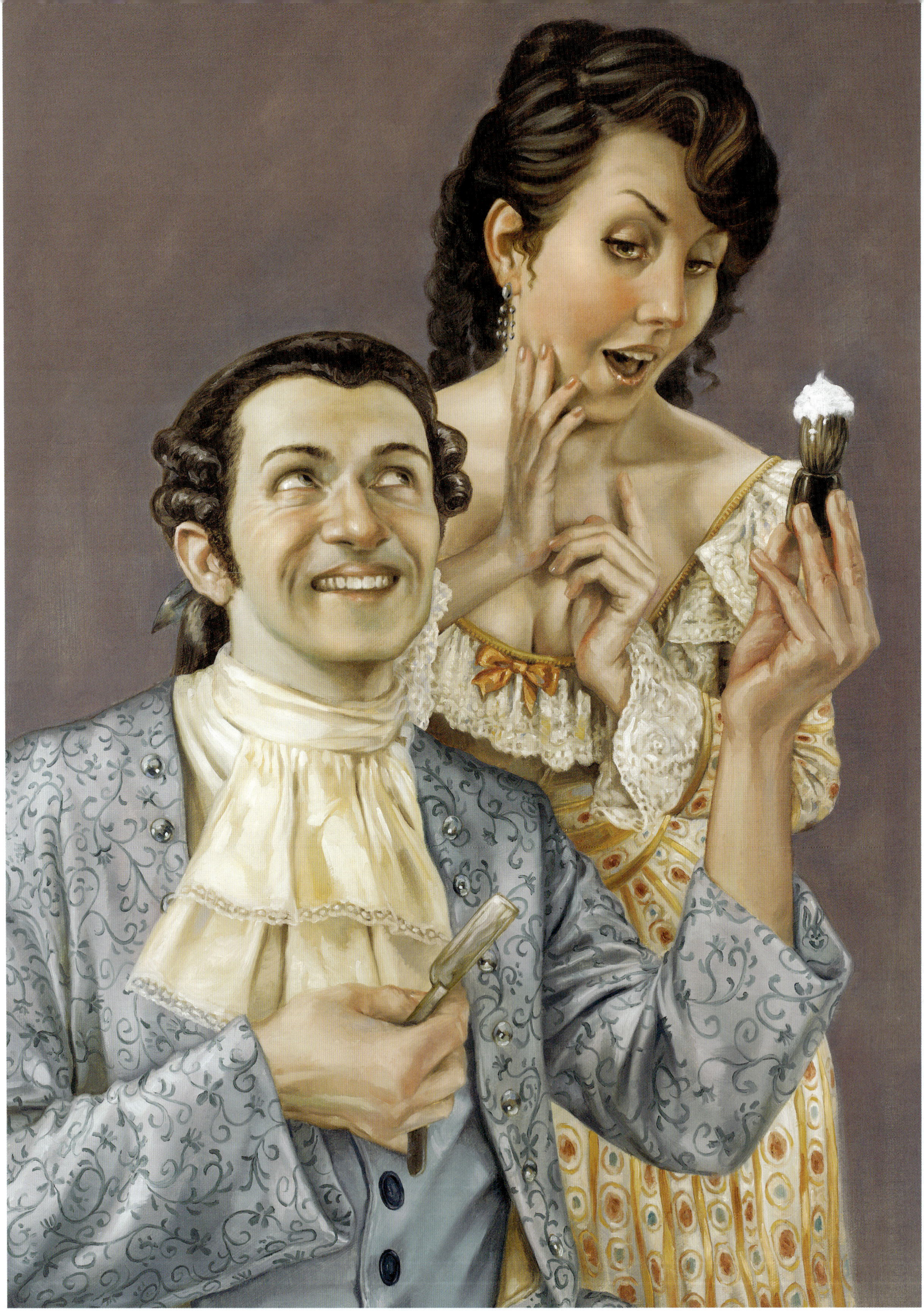

The Barber of Seville

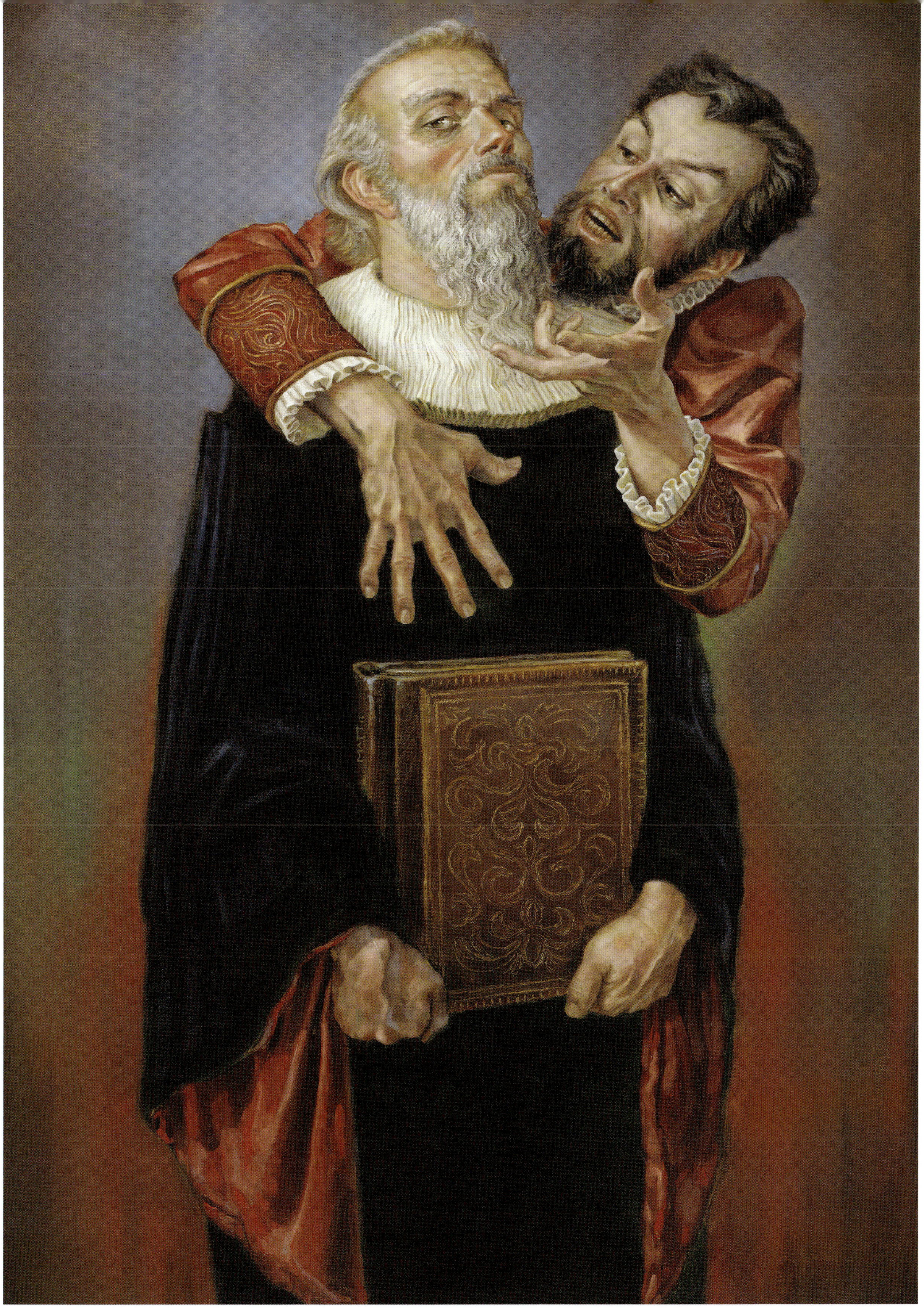

Faust

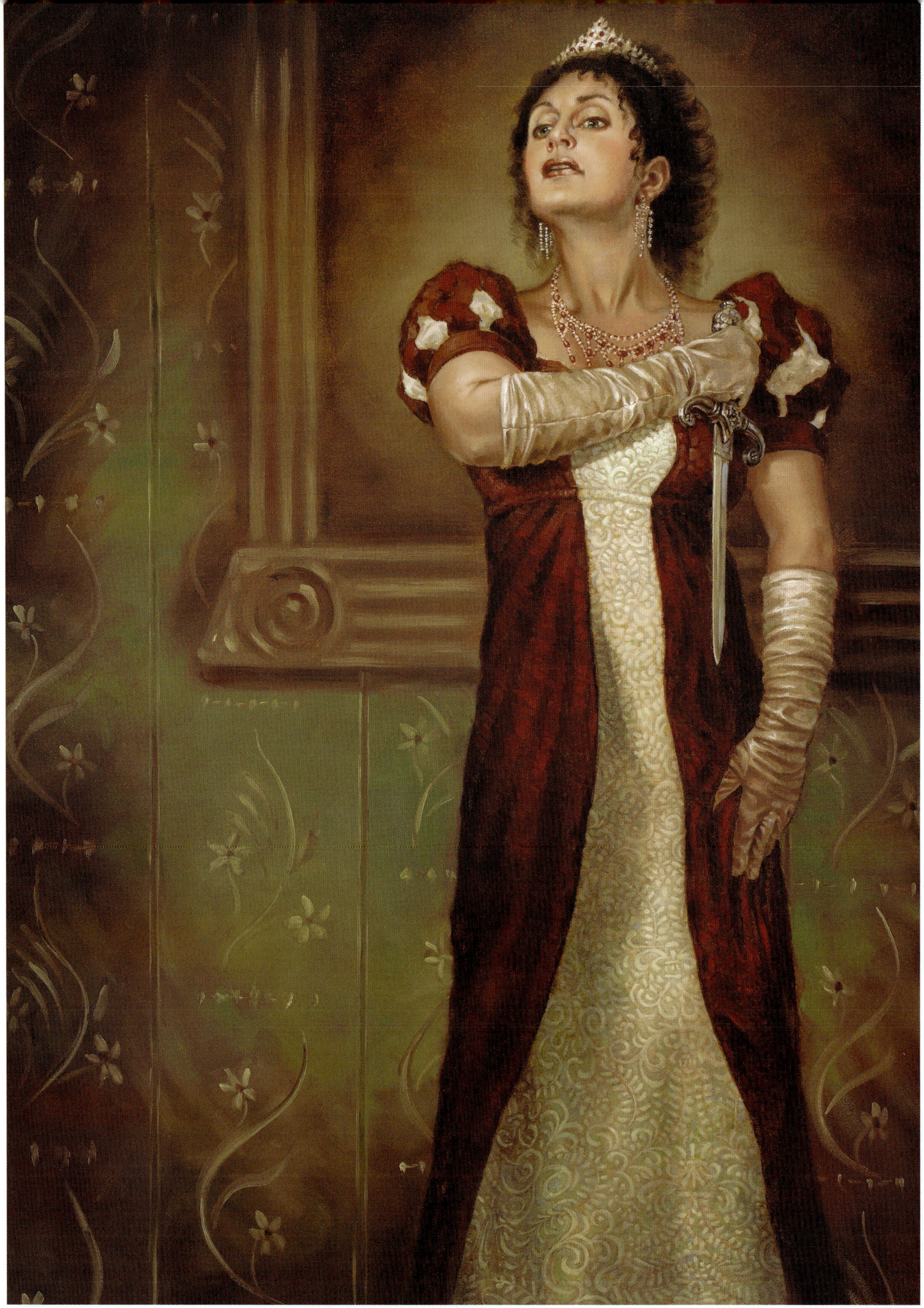

Tosca

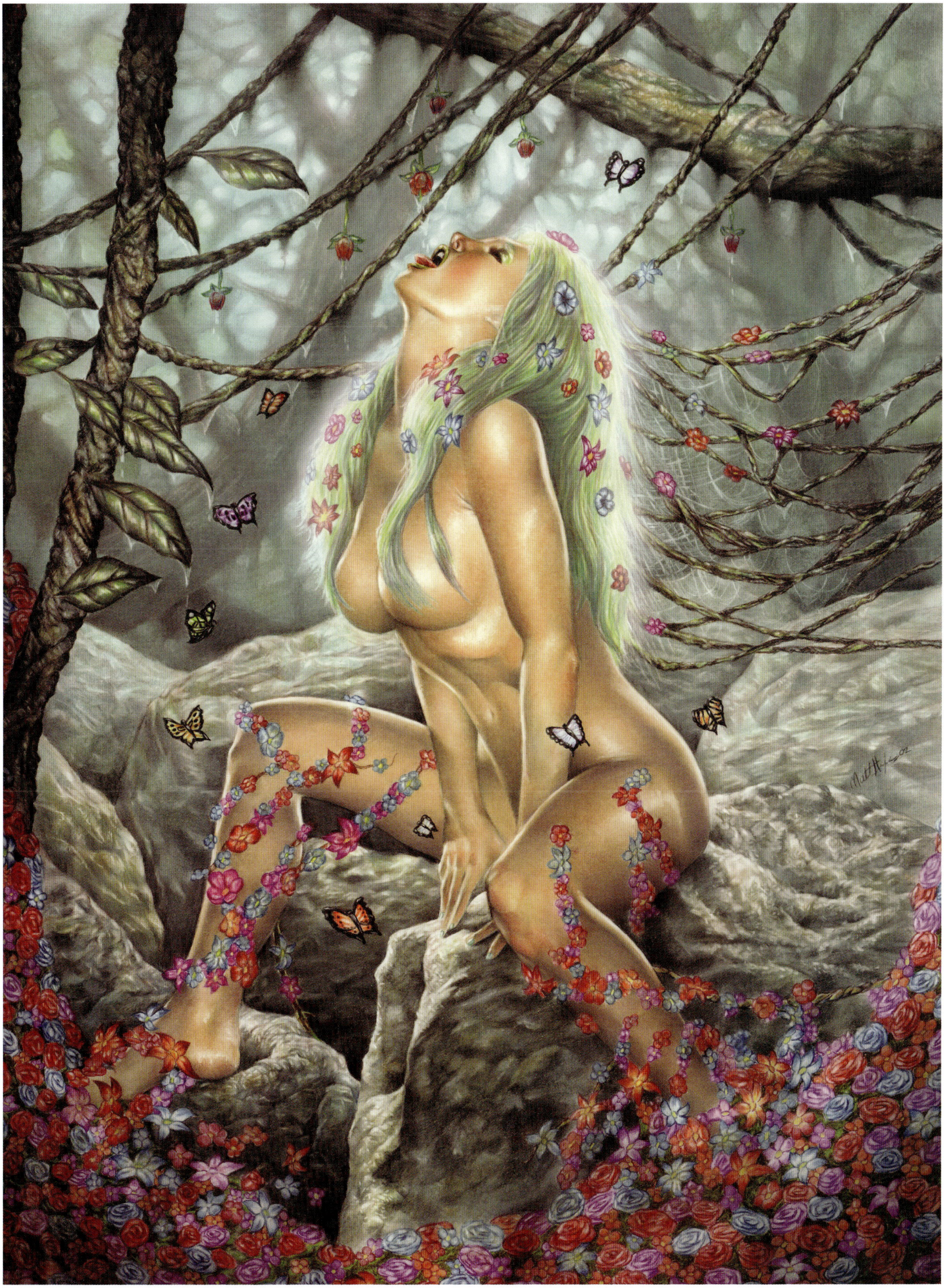

Tree

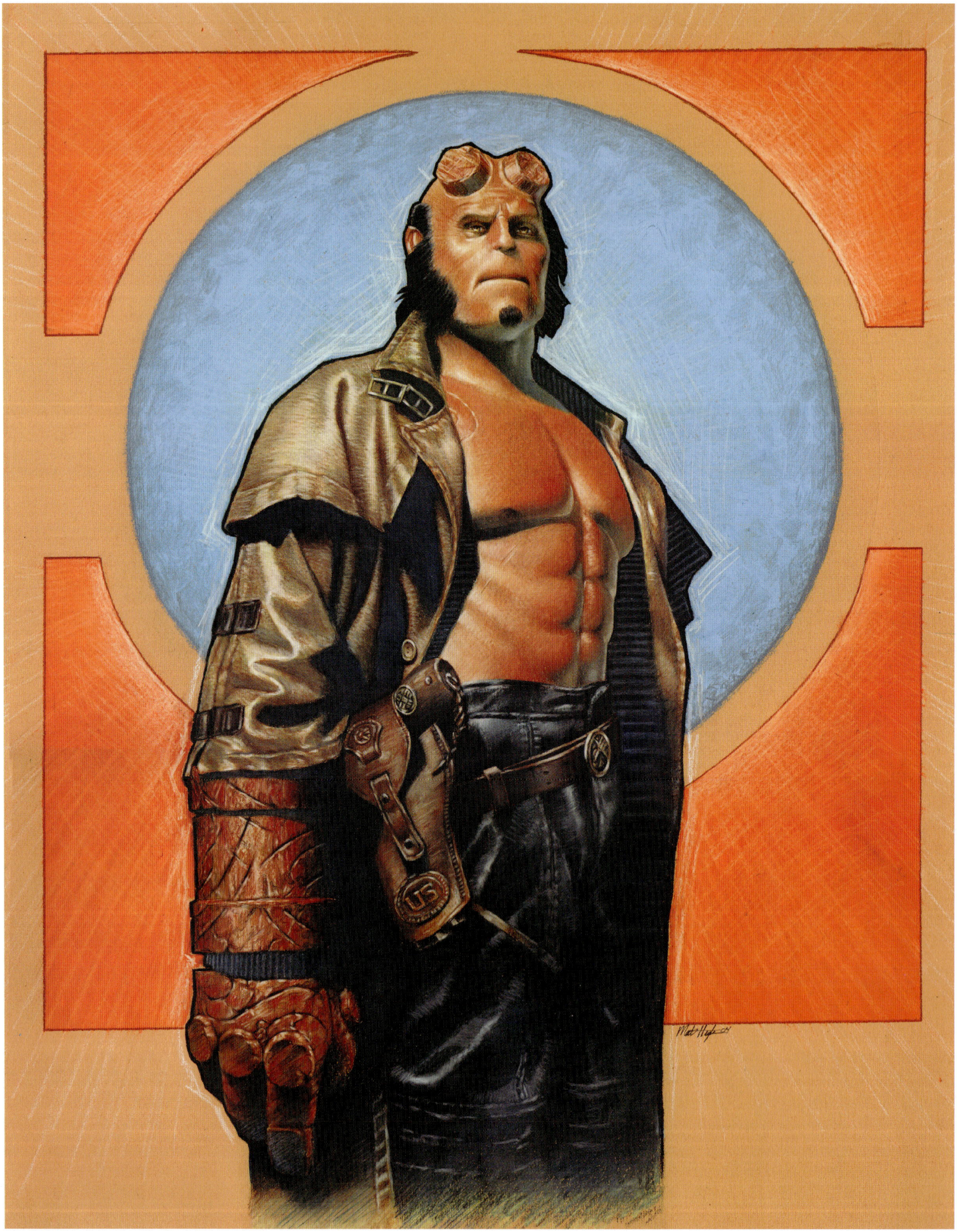

Hell Boy

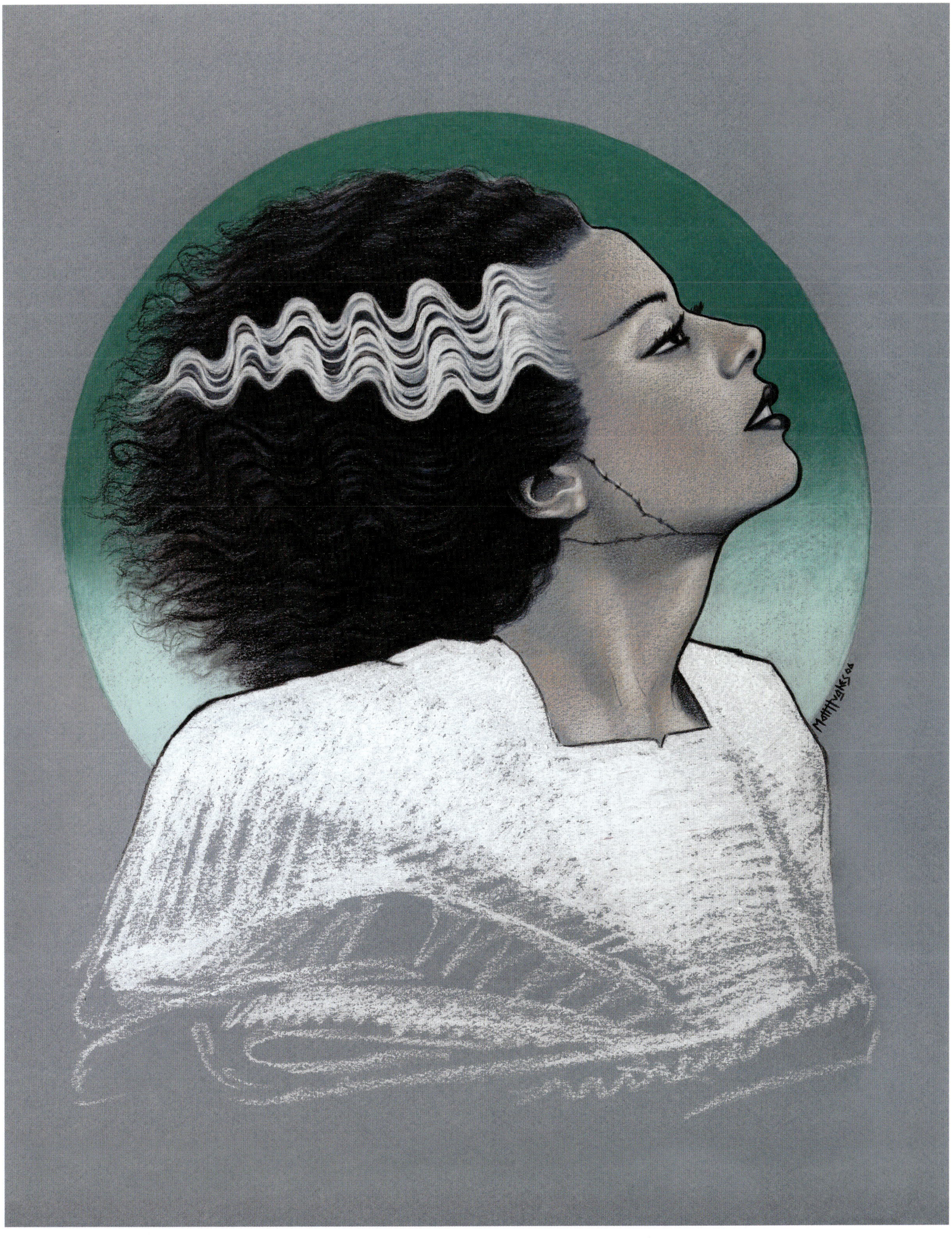

Bride

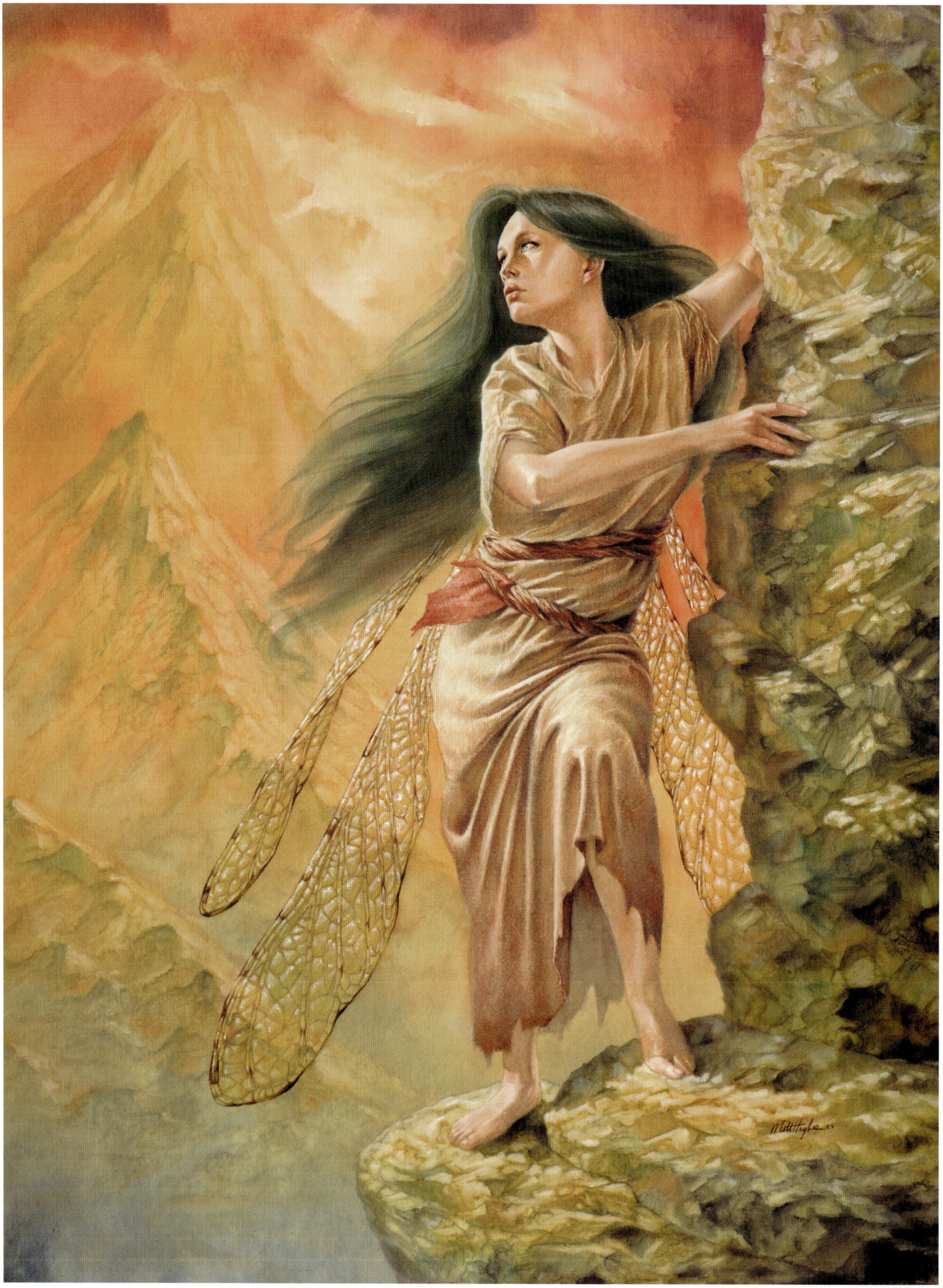

Falling

Preparation for Launch

Matt Hughes offers a step-by-step view of how he creates a painting

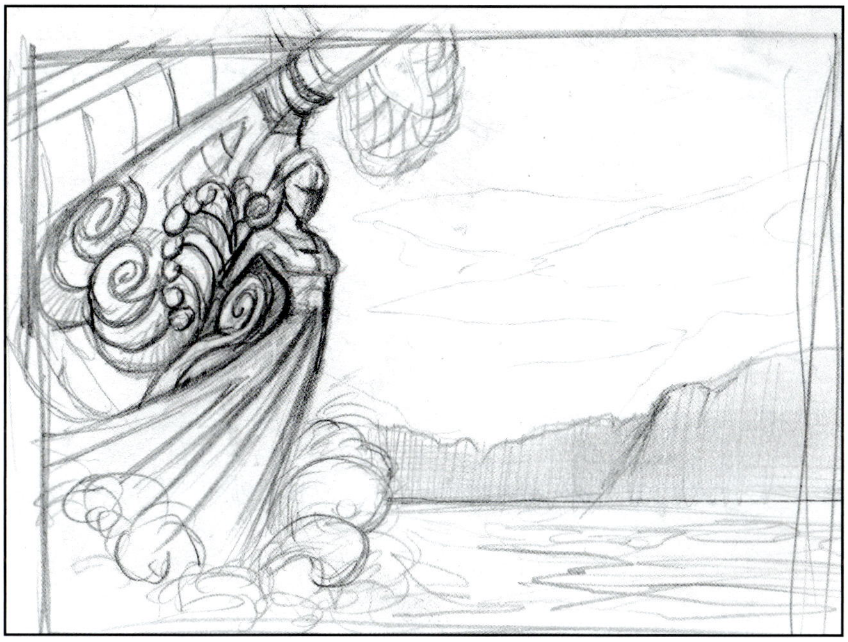

Step Concept:
At the initial stage I am presented with the material to illustrate. In this case, the material was a short story entitled *"Sonnets Made of Wood"* intended for publication in the magazine **Realms of Fantasy**. Once the material is reviewed I create a series of concept sketches that are presented to the client for approval and/or suggestions. With this particular story I felt an overall representation of the main character would be more appropriate then depicting a particular scene. Once the concept is approved I move on to the next phase of the project - the photo shoot.

Step Sketch:
Utilizing the photos that result from the shoot I produce a final line sketch, which is then forwarded to the client for final review. If there are no changes requested I enlarge the sketch to full size and transfer the sketch to the Vellum by hand using Colored Pencils (I use Clearprint Design Vellum). I find this to be the best Vellum for my needs. It is a cotton based material that carries a wax surface coating that works well with almost any medium including watercolor, ink, and oil paint.

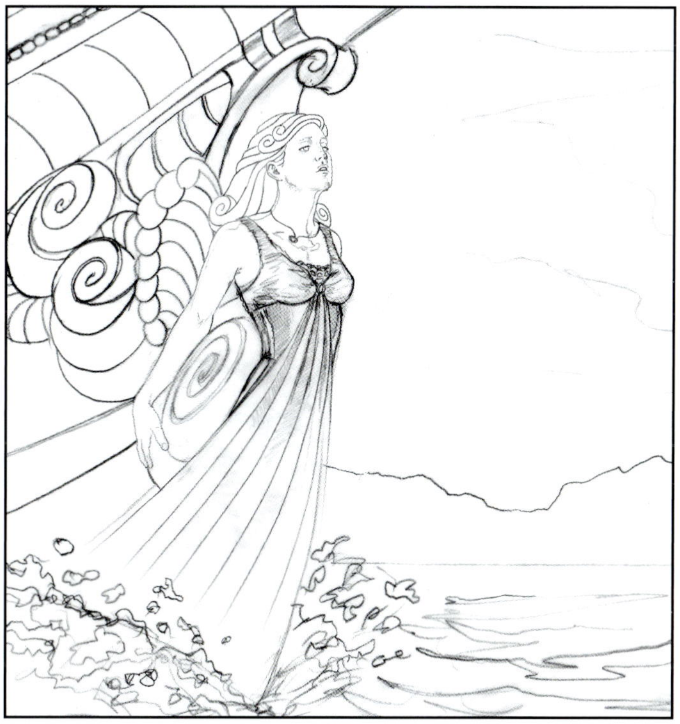

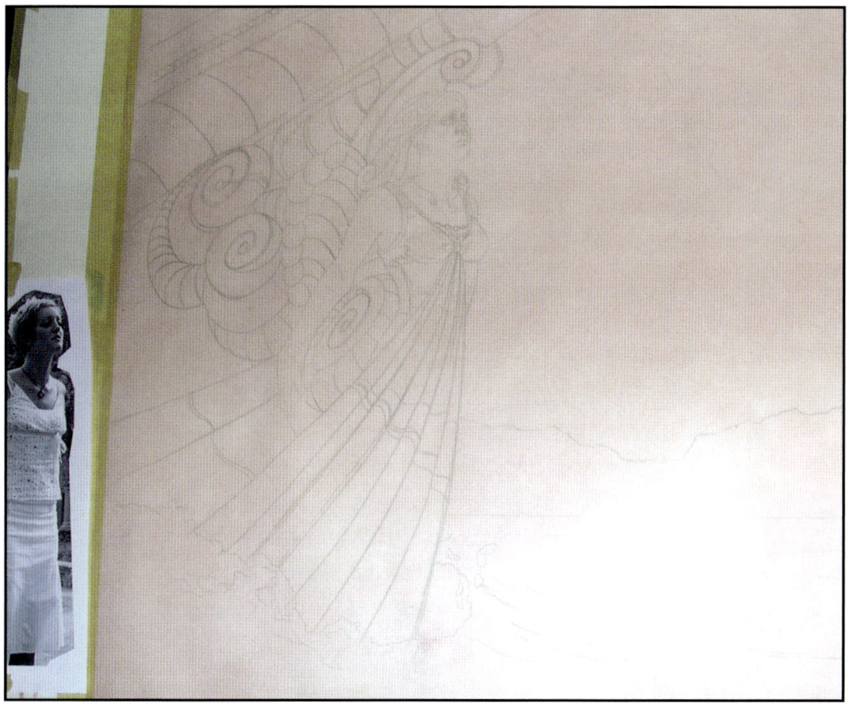

Step 1:
Once transferred to the final surface I "tint" the Vellum with an appropriate color to help with the overall color palette and to remove any white. In this case I used a light covering of Burnt Sienna. I always avoid working on a white surface as this can visually throw off the colors that are applied and can result in an undesirable effect. I primarily use Grumbacher Oil Paint for all of my painting. I find it has the best consistency of texture and drying time without breaking the bank. The color choices available seem to be more "earthy" than other lines of Oil Paint.

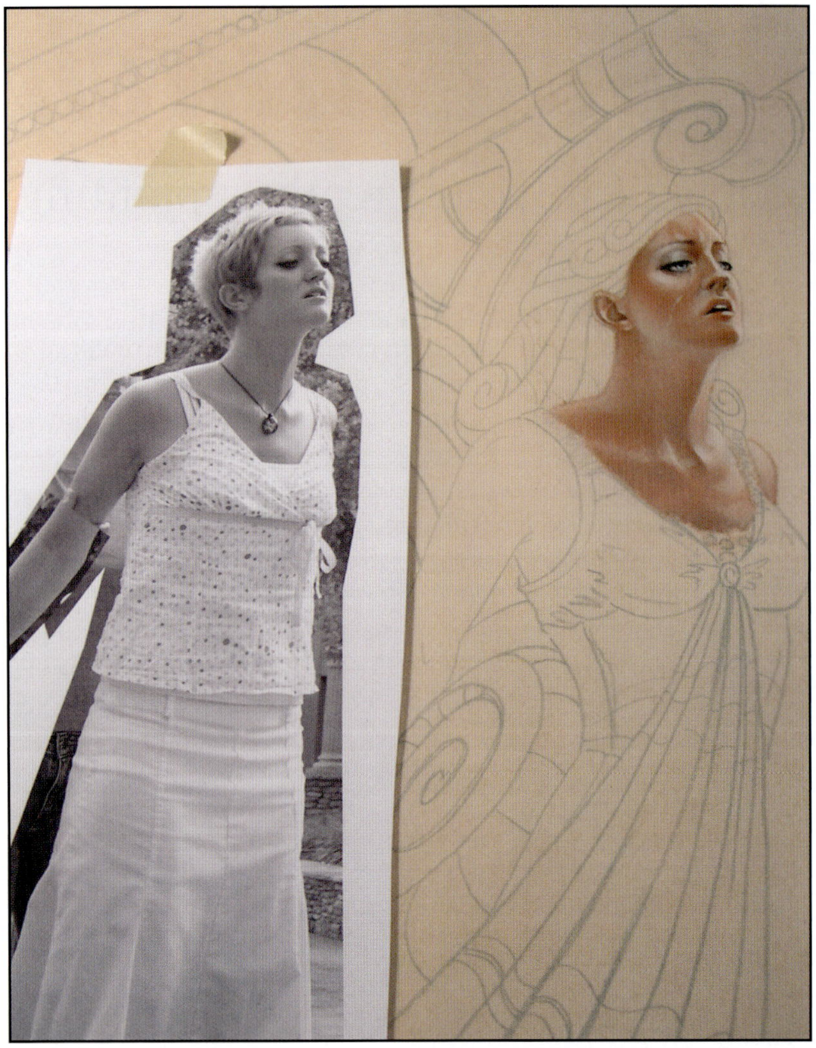

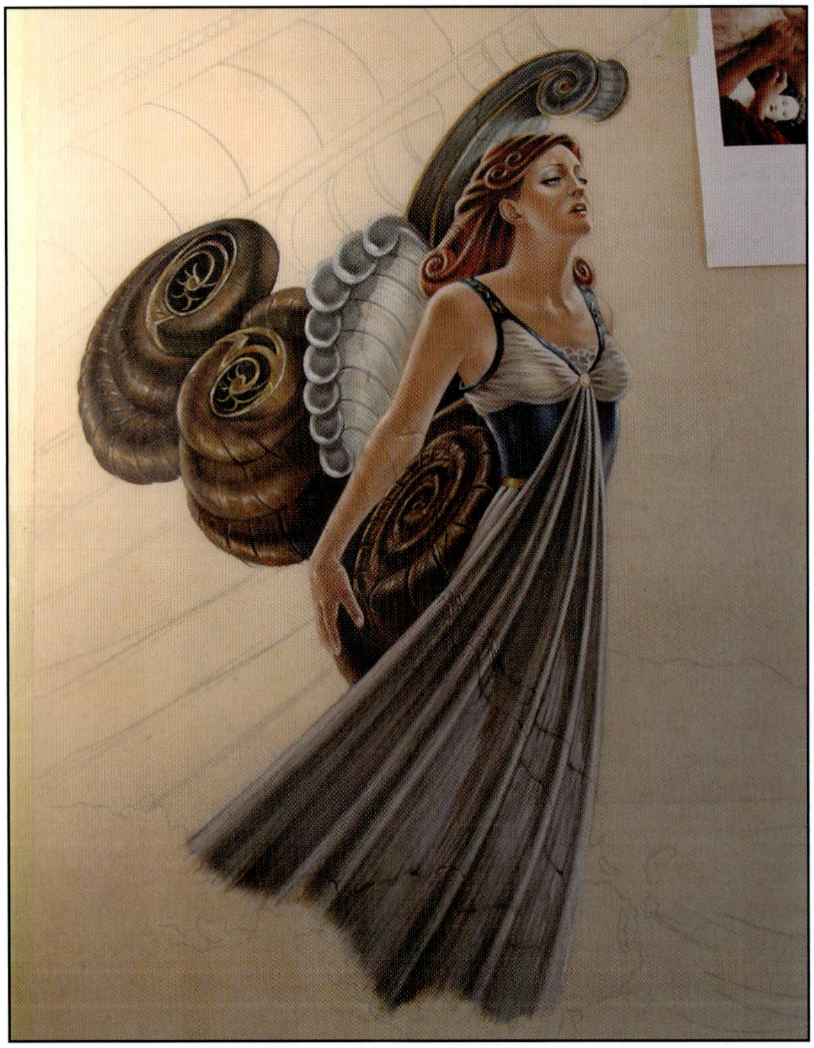

Step 2:
The first element that I always begin my final work with is the figures face. The face is always the focal point of any painting. It is human nature to always look directly at a human face when viewing anything including works of art. We judge the overall context of the piece by the expression and mood conveyed by the figure. Therefore, it has always been my first step. If the face does not convey my intended mood I will grab another piece of Vellum and start over.
I always convert all figure reference photos to grey in order to better understand lighting and shadows. With the photo reference close at hand I begin work on laying in the skin tones using Prismacolor Pencils. I have used Prismacolor Pencils for over a decade and have found them to be very reliable with consistent color and stability.
Since the skin tone in each illustration tends to be somewhat unique the combination of colors used varies. For this illustration I am attempting more of a classical outdoor feel. I am using several different blues (Slate Grey, Blue Slate, and Periwinkle) as well as some warm reds and browns (Peach, Sienna Brown, Terra Cotta, Blush Pink, and Mineral Orange). The process for my colored pencil work is a series of layering that involves laying down several colors, blending with White or a blending pencil, then laying down more colors, then more White, etc. until I reach my desired color. It is really a discovery process and is influenced by everything from the pressure used on the pencil to the sharpness of the pencil. You need to be careful, though. With colored pencil you tend to reach a point where you will be unable to lay any more pencil down due to wax build up. Once you reach this stage do not try and force more color on the vellum. It will only result in a rutty look.

Step 3:
As I continue to work I reference other elements that will assist me with the illustration (notice the reference photos at the top right). I reference classic ship objects in order help insure a classical look to the piece.
Since much of the ship required a very detailed approach I decided to produce the majority of it using colored pencil. There is a softness that can be achieved with colored pencil that is very unique to this medium. This can be a help or a hindrance depending on your desired end result. Since the main character in the story is slowly turning into wood and becoming part of the vessel I needed to convey this transformation within the figure. I accomplished this by adding in details such as wood grain and cracks into her skin to give the feeling of the transformation. The most effective representation of this transformation can be seen in the figures hair. Much like my photo references I interpreted her hair with block shapes and grooves rather then realistic hair. I left the face, neck and shoulders more realistic in order to support her original human state. Per the story, I added the tear on her cheek.

Step 4:
Now that the ship is complete I move on to the background and foreground water. This stage will be accomplished with Oil Paint. Note the color study at the top of the drawing table. By laying in basic colors onto a small copy of the line sketch I have a sort of road map to help guide me regarding color choices. Since I primed my Vellum with a light Burnt Sienna application (refer to step 1) it will be much easier for me to accomplish the classical look in the sky and ocean.

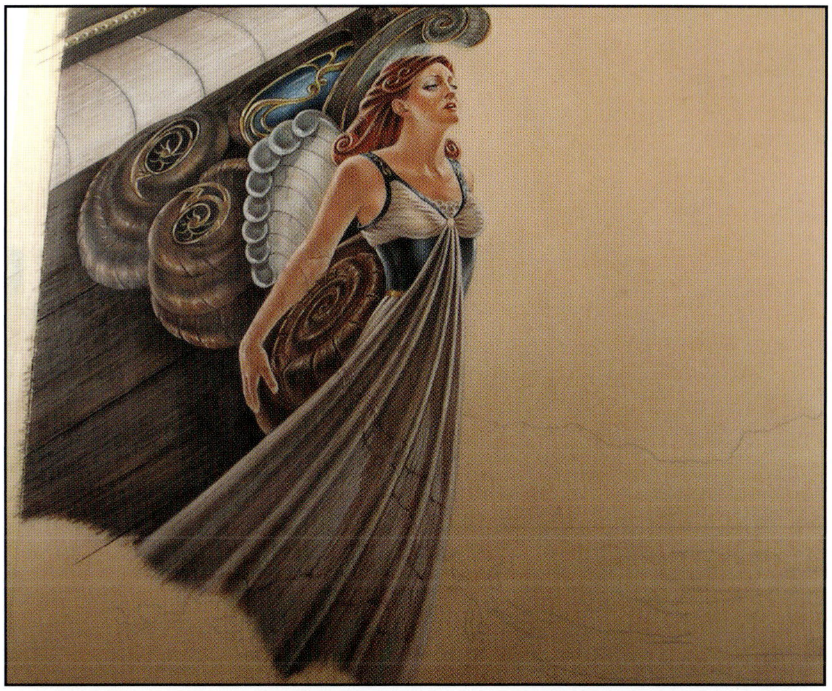

Step 5:
This step involves working fairly quickly with the Oil Paint. Oil Paint tends to dry rather fast on Vellum so you need to be sure of the colors you use. Vellum is not very forgiving. Again, note the many reference photos placed around my painting. I am constantly referring to these pictures for inspiration and guidance.
Since I am such a student of the Pre-Raphaelite age I tend to utilize colors in similar ways. By applying similar colors "wet" I achieve more of a classical look to the piece.
Also, notice at the top I have added tape to help keep the sharp edge of the ship (I'm sure the airbrush artists out there can relate to this technique!). If you have a similar need for such a mask be sure to remove some of the stickiness from the tape. Otherwise you will remove specs of colored pencil once you remove the mask. If you find the paint very dry when laying it down on the vellum try applying a thin wash of linseed oil first. This should help make the vellum more accepting of the paint. Be careful not to apply too much, though. The Vellum does not absorb the linseed oil as easily or as quickly as canvas or board. If you apply too much it will cause the color to run or drip down off of the surface.
Next I will lay in the mountains in the distance.

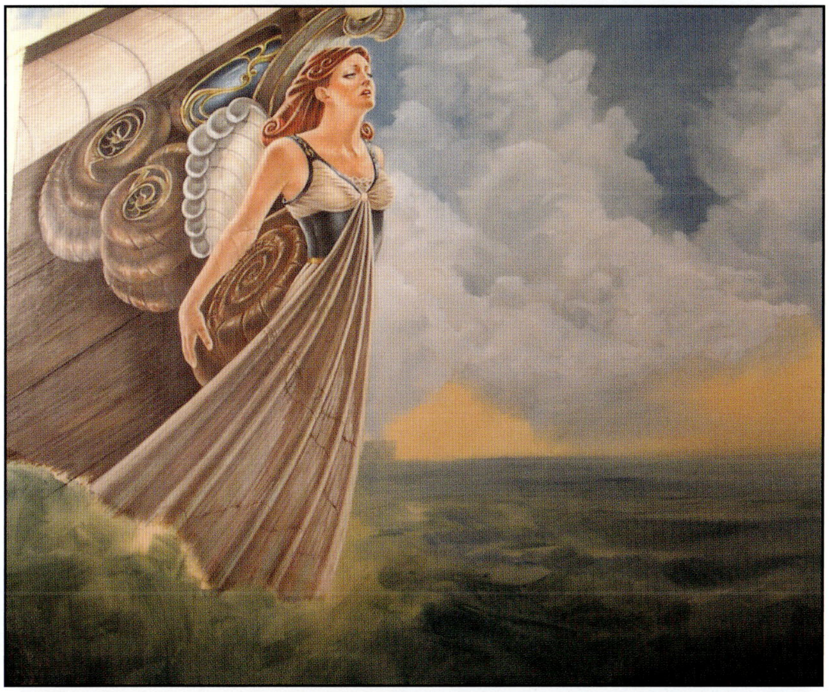

Step 6:
Now that the mountains have been added we get more of a feel for the atmosphere. By utilizing similar colors that are also used in the sky and sea I was able to place the mountains in rather quickly and produce a unified feel. The sharpness of the mountains also helped to push the clouds back further. Notice that my initial tinting of Burnt Sienna that was applied to the Vellum is still showing through. Now with the mask remove on the upper part of the ship I will go back into the ship and add more contrast where needed.
After I have added more contrast to the pencil work I will finish the painting by adding in the white foam and the crashing waves. I accomplish the "vein" effect of the foam by laying in fairly thick thin lines of white paint on the still damp ocean. This results in a series of blends and reapplications of paint. Once the "veins" have been added all that is lacking is the final touch of the crashing waves hitting the boa of the ship

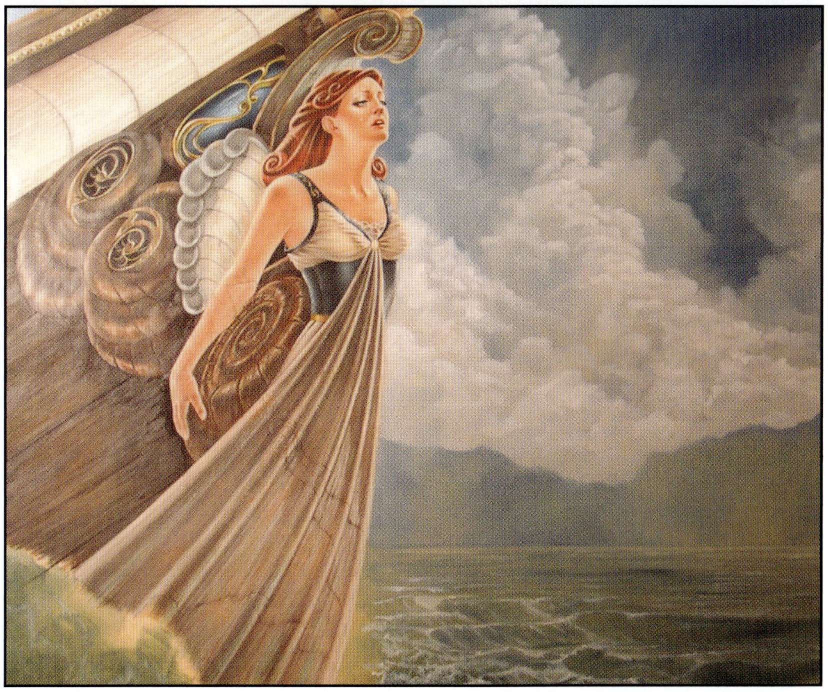

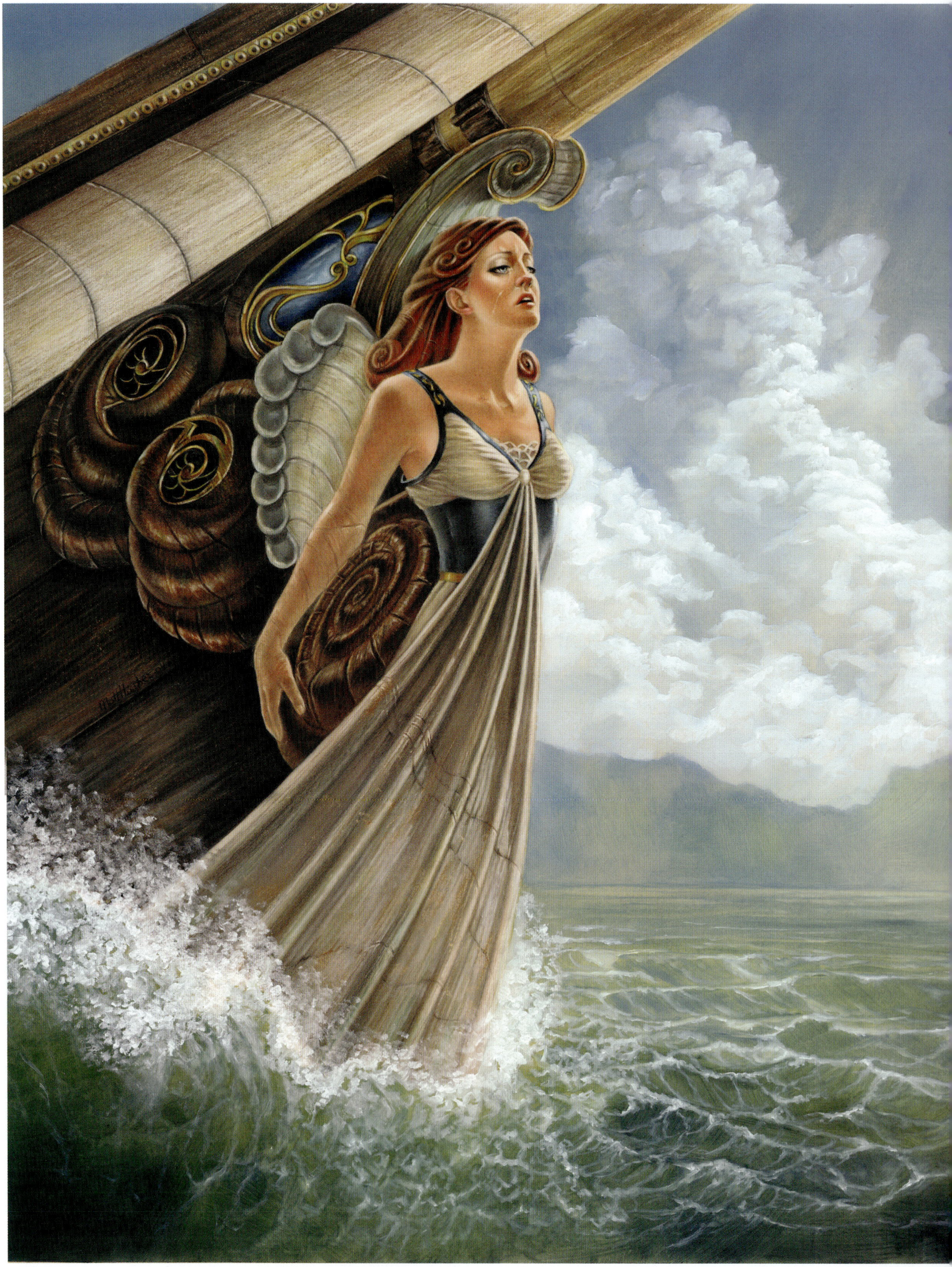

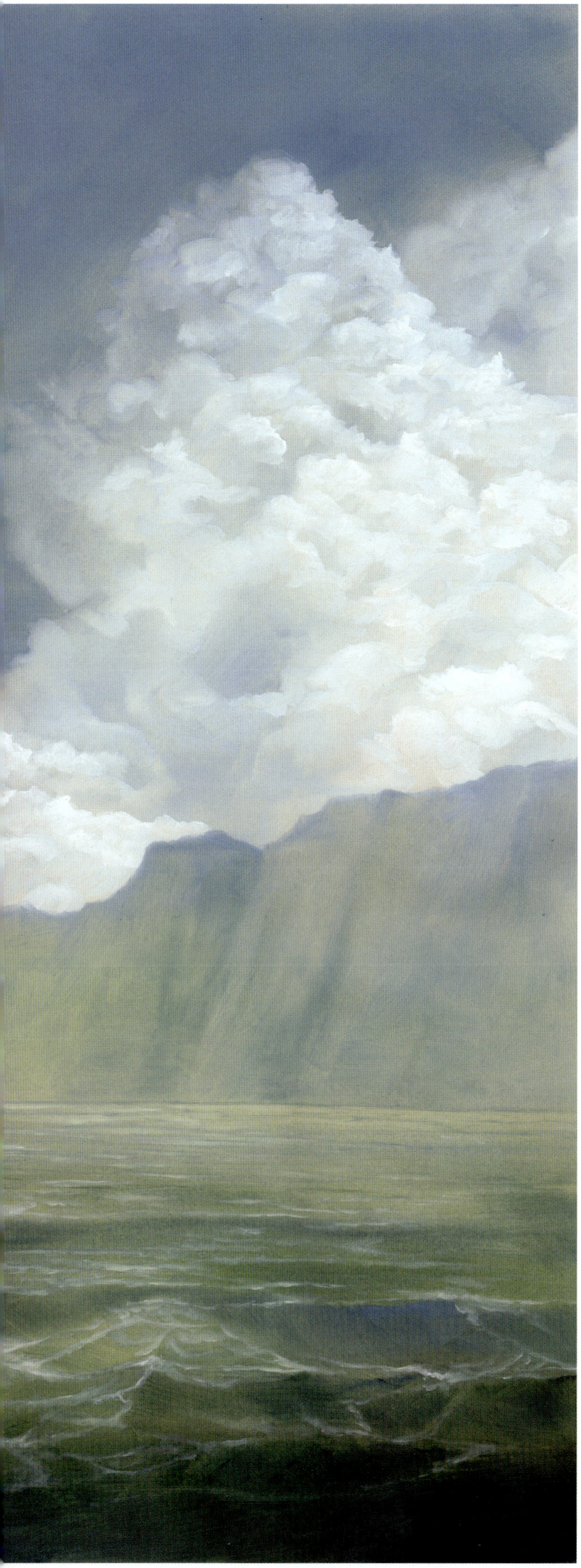

Step 7:
The final illustration as it appeared in the publication. Once dried, I sprayed the finished piece with several thin layers of Fixative to protect the colored pencil and help bring out the contrast of the piece. By spraying the pencil with the Fixative you help to eliminate the "fog" that will appear with colored pencil work. This "fog" is a result of the wax in the pencil and, if not treated, will continue to get worse over time. It is not damaging to the illustration since it can be treated at any time with fixative to remove this "fog". Once completed, the final is scanned and color corrected to better match the original. This final digital file is then delivered to the client ready for print. I have found that most clients in the industry prefer and appreciate the final illustration being delivered to them in a digital format ready for print. It certainly saves time and actually gives you a few more days to reach that tight deadline.

To learn more about Matt and his work please visit his website at **www.matthughesart.com**

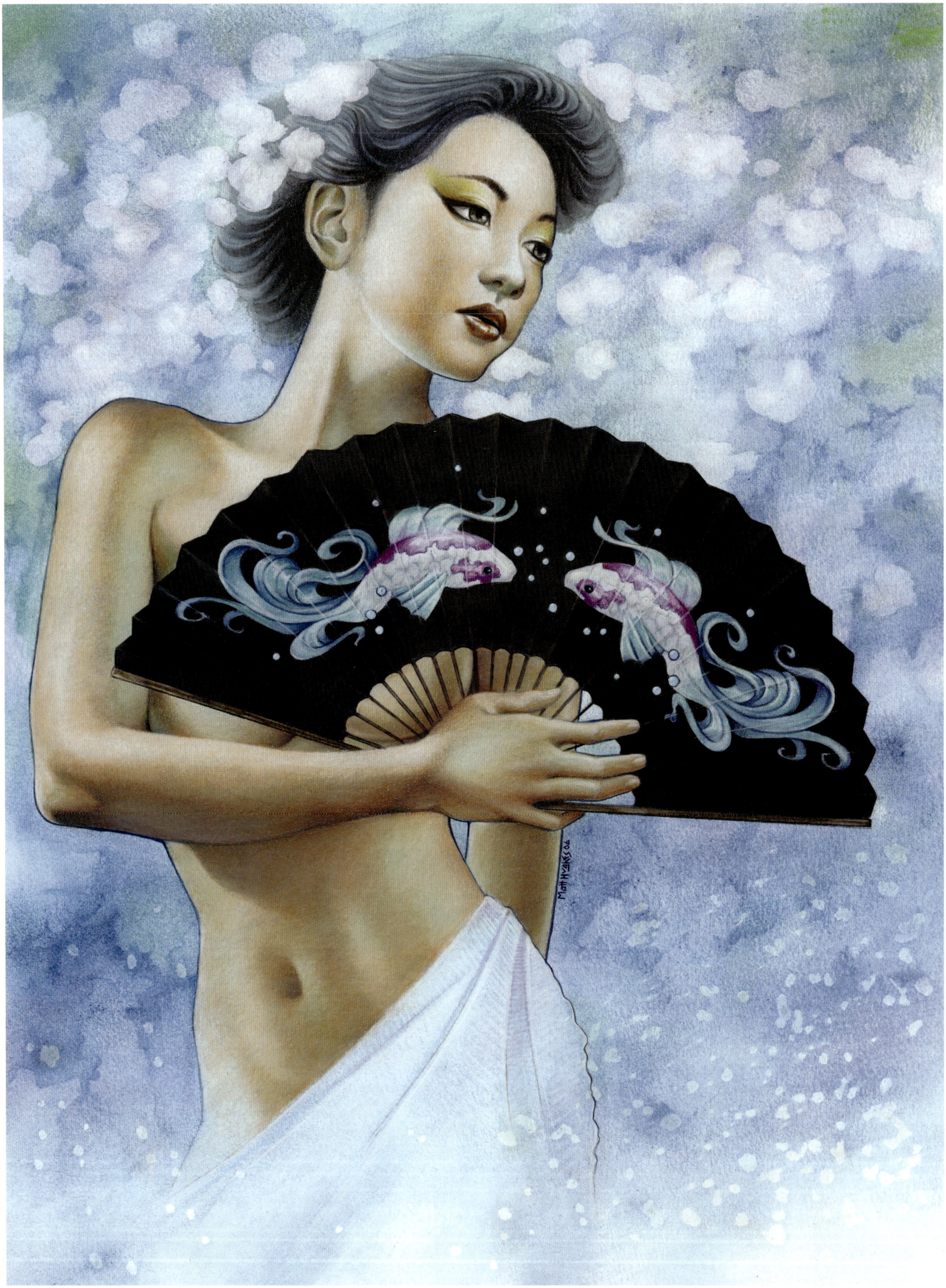

Water